UPPER PRIMARY

THE ENVIRONMENT
Promoting Sustainability

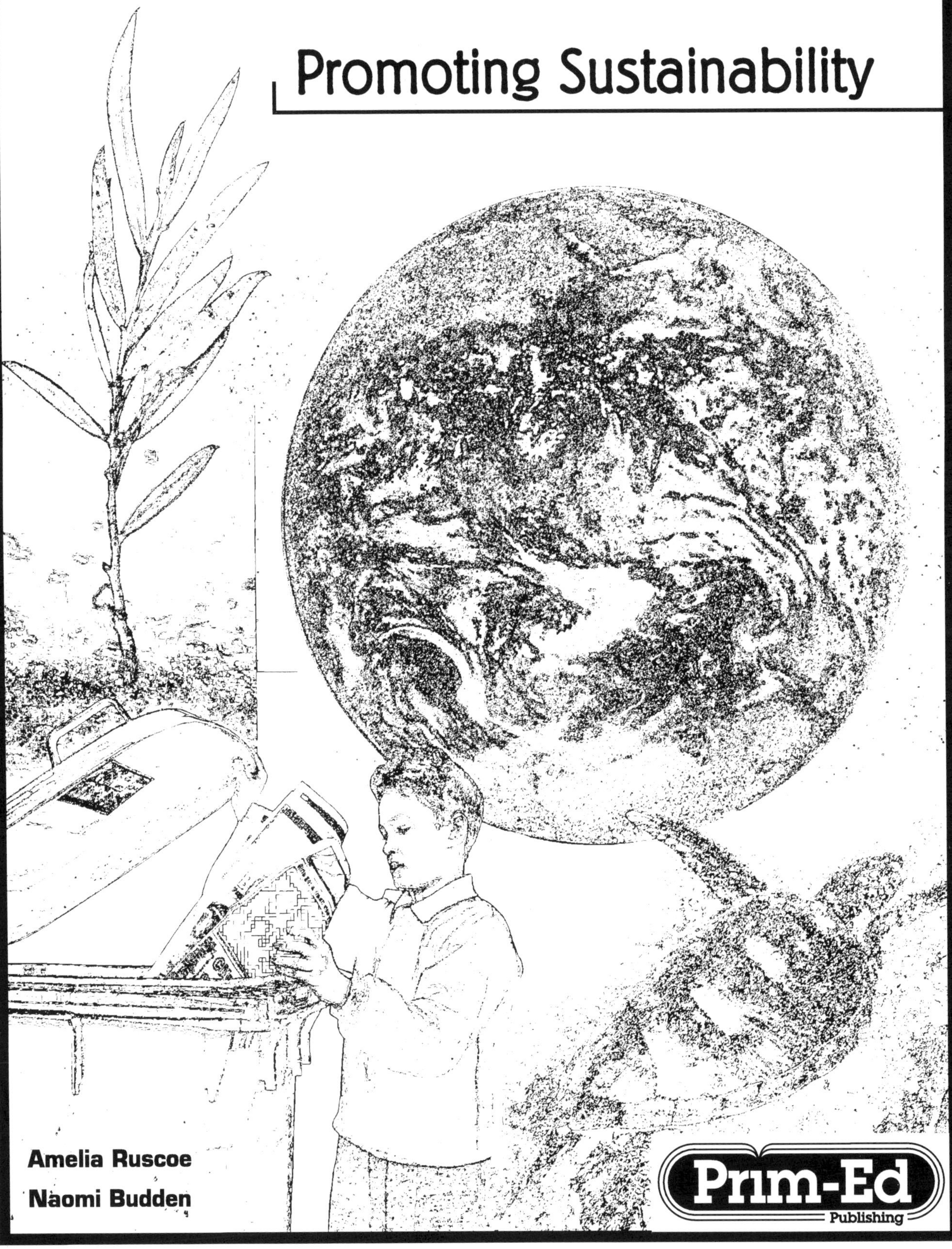

Amelia Ruscoe
Naomi Budden

Prim-Ed Publishing

0550C

The environment—Upper primary
Prim-Ed Publishing

Published in 2007 by Prim-Ed Publishing
Reprinted under licence by Prim-Ed Publishing 2007

Copyright Amelia Ruscoe and Naomi Budden 2003

This master may only be reproduced by the original purchaser for use with their class(es). The publisher prohibits the loaning or onselling of this master for the purposes of reproduction.

ISBN 978-1-84654-103-2
PR–0550

Additional titles available in this series:
The environment—Lower primary
The environment—Middle primary

View all pages online.

Email Address: sales@prim-ed.com
Home Page: www.prim-ed.com

Internet websites
In some cases, websites or specific URLs may be recommended. While these are checked and rechecked at the time of publication, the publisher has no control over any subsequent changes which may be made to webpages. It is *strongly* recommended that the class teacher checks *all* URLs before allowing pupils to access them.

Copyright Notice

Blackline masters or copy masters are published and sold with a limited copyright. This copyright allows publishers to provide teachers and schools with a wide range of learning activities without copyright being breached. This limited copyright allows the purchaser to make sufficient copies for use within their own education institution. The copyright is not transferable, nor can it be onsold. Following these instructions is not essential but will ensure that you, as the purchaser, have evidence of legal ownership to the copyright if inspection occurs.
For your added protection in the case of copyright inspection, please complete the form below. Retain this form, the complete original document and the invoice or receipt as proof of purchase.

Name of Purchaser:_____   Date of Purchase:_____

Supplier:_____   School Order# (if applicable):_____

Signature of Purchaser:_____

The environment

Foreword

The environment provides a comprehensive overview of issues relating to the state of our natural environment. The book is structured so as to challenge pupils to consider the consequences of human activities upon the environment and to take positive steps towards building a sustainable lifestyle and a balanced approach to living within their environment.

Each unit equips pupils with information about a different aspect of our environment, including natural resources, pollution, recycling, energy, biodiversity and conservation. An informational text page with accompanying word study and comprehension activities is also provided with each unit to complement activities which focus on science, geography and health education.

Comprehensive background information, teachers notes, answers and additional activities are also included to support the teaching of each unit.

Books in this series include: *The environment* – Lower primary
The environment – Middle primary
The environment – Upper primary

Each book in this series is also provided in digital format on the accompanying CD.

Contents

Teachers notes .... ii – iii

Lifestyle and the environment
Reading – Informational text .... 2 – 3
Reading – Word study/comprehension .... 4 – 5
Geography – This is the life... or is it? .... 6 – 7
Geography – Lifestyle comparison .... 8 – 9

Smart resources
Reading – Informational text .... 10 – 11
Reading – Word study/comprehension .... 12 – 13
Science/Technology – Resources with a future .... 14 – 15
Geography – What happens in 50 years? .... 16 – 17

Can we run out of fish?
Reading – Informational text .... 18 – 19
Reading – Word study/comprehension .... 20 – 21
Science – Why we need fish .... 22 – 23
Geography – Good fishermen .... 24 – 25

A tree named Luna
Reading – Informational text .... 26 – 27
Reading – Word study/comprehension .... 28 – 29
Science – Ancient trees – not just for me .... 30 – 31
Geography – Stopping the rot .... 32 – 33

Life in a greenhouse
Reading – Informational text .... 34 – 35
Reading – Word study/comprehension .... 36 – 37
Science – The greenhouse experiment .... 38 – 39
Geography – Simple solutions .... 40 – 41

Biodiversity
Reading – Informational text .... 42 – 43
Reading – Word study/comprehension .... 44 – 45
Science – A scientific language .... 46 – 47
Geography – The nature revolution .... 48 – 49

Threatened species
Reading – Informational text .... 50 – 51
Reading – Word study/comprehension .... 52 – 53
Science – Habitats in a rainforest – close up .... 54 – 55
Science – Quarantine .... 56 – 57

Conserving Timbertown
Reading – Informational text .... 58 – 59
Reading – Word study/comprehension .... 60 – 61
Science – Natural air fresheners .... 62 – 63
Geography – Consider the consequences .... 64 – 65

Is it a whale or a shark?
Reading – Informational text .... 66 – 67
Reading – Word study/comprehension .... 68 – 69
Science – The status of wildlife .... 70 – 71
Geography – Swimming with whale sharks .... 72 – 73

Natural ecosystems
Reading – Informational text .... 74 – 75
Reading – Word study/comprehension .... 76 – 77
Science – Special plants of special places .... 78 – 79
Geography – Australia's ecosystems .... 80 – 81

Look at us now!
Reading – Informational text .... 82 – 83
Reading – Word study/comprehension .... 84 – 85
Science – Room for improvement .... 86 – 87
Literacy – Information for change .... 88 – 89

Getting your hands dirty
Reading – Informational text .... 90 – 91
Reading – Word study/comprehension .... 92 – 93
Geography – Attracting wildlife .... 94 – 95
Health – In the media .... 96 – 97

Glossary .... 98 – 101

Teachers notes

The environment

The environment has been designed to encourage pupils to investigate aspects of our environment which are under threat as a result of human activities and to promote an understanding of the progress that is being made towards creating a sustainable planet. Aspects addressed include:

- natural resource use
- biodiversity
- recycling
- renewable energy sources
- pollution
- conservation

The material can be taught as whole units of work which progress logically to create a knowledge base for pupils to approach more challenging environment issues. Alternatively, the activities within each unit can be used to complement existing environment-based programmes.

Each book contains 12 units. Each unit is divided into four sections with an icon denoting the focus of each activity.

Reading – informational text about the topic

Reading – word study/comprehension

Science-related activity

Geography or health-related activity

Background information provides the teacher with relevant information additional to the pupil page.

An **objective(s)** explains what the pupil is expected to demonstrate through completing the activities.

Curriculum links appropriate to each country are provided across the main learning area.

The first two pages of each unit include a '**Reading Focus**' passage for the pupils to read either in a whole-class situation, in small focus groups, independently or as part of a homework assignment.

Discussion questions encourage the pupils to comprehend, assess and form opinions about what they have read.

Websites relevant to the topic are included.

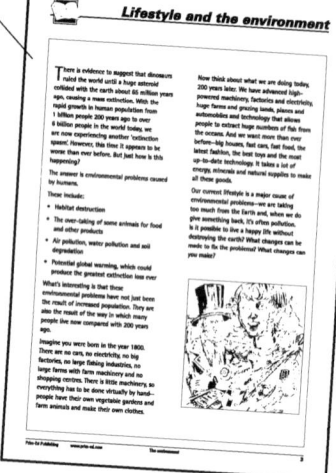

Answers are provided on the accompanying teachers notes.

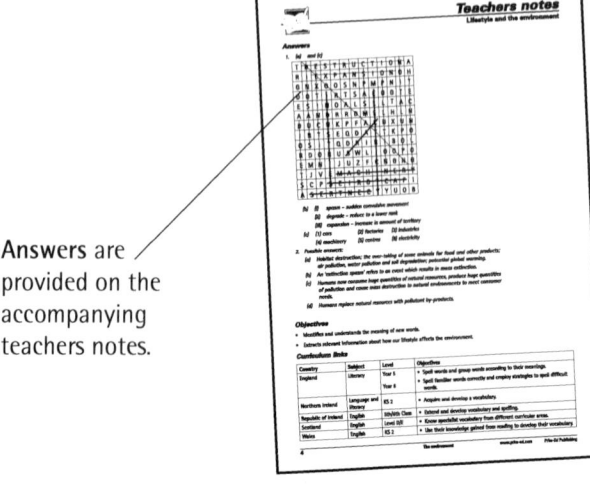

The third and fourth pages of each unit include **word study** and **comprehension** activities based on the text.

Pupils are required to clarify definitions and identify 10 words and their spelling within the text.

Comprehension questions are provided to assist in developing an understanding of the concepts being introduced.

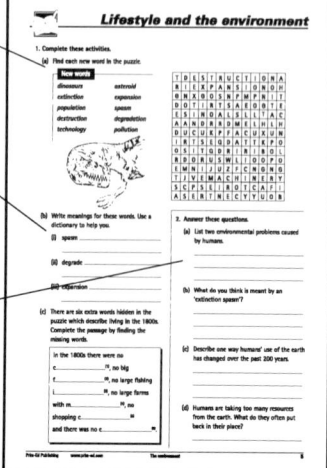

ii — The environment — www.prim-ed.com — Prim-Ed Publishing

Teachers notes

The environment

The final four pages of each unit include two science, geography or health education activities.

These activities aim to complement learning about the unit topic by encouraging pupils to investigate aspects of their environment in a practical manner and, in some cases, to assess the management of the environment of both their local environment and the earth as a whole. The activities aim to have the pupils employ prior knowledge, along with the new information they have learnt, to make informed decisions about their environment and how its natural resources can be sustained for the benefit of their own and future generations.

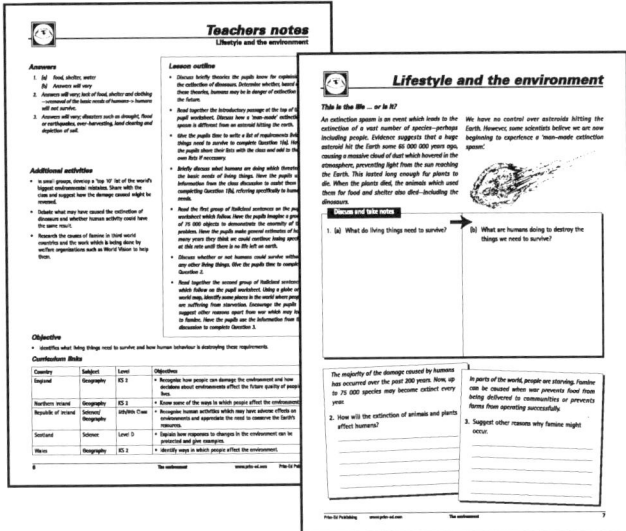

Each science, geography and health education activity is supported by detailed teachers notes.

Lesson outlines include guided questioning, discussion points, and additional teaching strategies to ensure the pupils achieve maximum understanding.

Objective(s) and **curriculum links** are also provided.

Additional activities can be used in conjunction with the pupil worksheets or as a basis for further lessons on the same conceptual understanding.

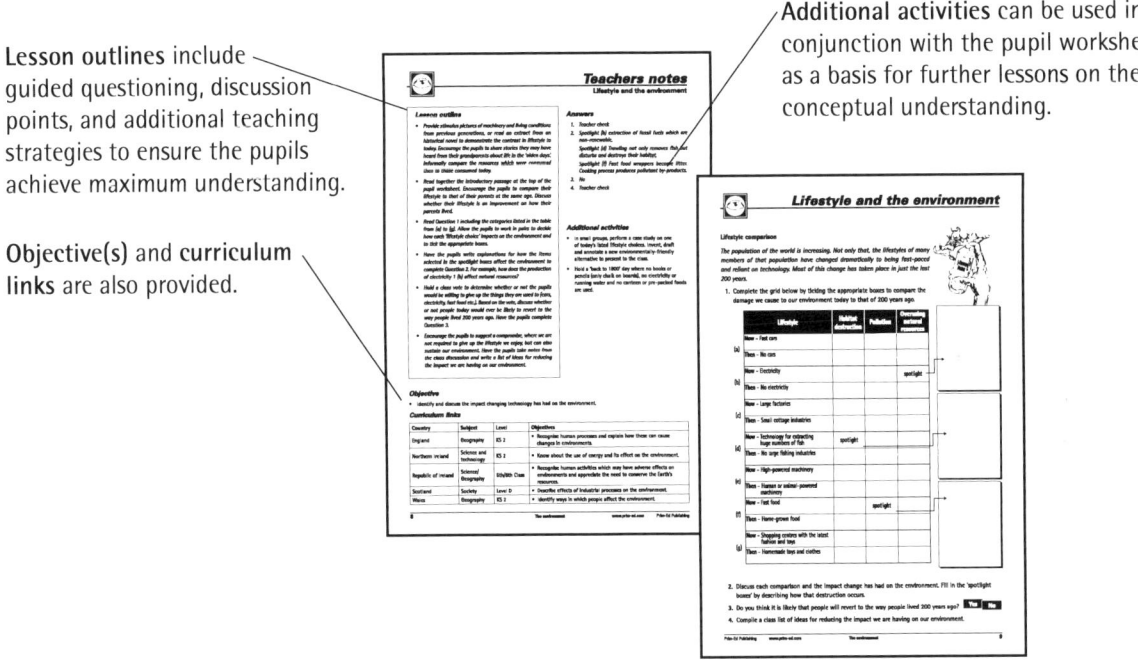

Each book in this series is also provided in digital format. Using this format as an alternative to the print edition provides the following advantages.

(i) Not all pages require photocopying. In some situations, displaying the page on an interactive whiteboard provides sufficient detail and direction to enable successful completion of activity or provision of information.

(ii) The digital edition allows you to print directly to your printer.

(iii) The digital edition allows the page to be moved around the interactive whiteboard screen as required.

(iv) The digital edition allows the page to be zoomed in/out to allow focus on specific locations or activities.

(v) The digital edition allows for discrete sections to be screened by the use of slides.

Teachers notes
Lifestyle and the environment

Background information

Many people look at the increasing population of the Earth as the reason behind environmental problems; more people equal more destruction of natural areas and more pollution. This maybe true, but what compounds the problem is an enormous increase in consumerism in developed countries. When we understand this concept, we also understand that humans affect the earth at different rates.

The impact of one human can be a lot more than that of another. Generally speaking, individual people in less-developed countries have less of an environmental impact on the earth than individuals in well-developed countries. This is because they consume much less in terms of energy and other natural resources. However, their total populations are usually a lot higher than in well-developed countries, which may affect some of the imbalance.

This combined effect of population multiplied by consumption is called an ecological footprint. An interesting social comparison is to imagine if all six billion people in the world had the same standard of living and consumption levels afforded to people in the western world. To do this we would require the natural resources of three worlds. In other words, at the current world population, for us to be able to live the way we do, requires that most of the world's people live a far less consumptive life—what we consider to be a lower standard of living.

This is a very interesting situation if you believe that all people should have the same rights to the world's resources. However, because resource management practices are often unsustainable, there would have to be a dramatic lifestyle shift away from consumerism before all people could enjoy a comfortable standard of living.

Although this sounds equitable in theory, if the world is to truly work towards fairer natural resource use in the future, a multi-faceted approach of sustainable resource management, combined with a reduction in both population and consumerism, may be the only way this could ever be achieved.

Discussion points

- When would be a better time to live? Now or 200 years ago?
- Are you doing all you can to help the environment?
- Can you make a difference?

Websites

http://www.populationinstitute.org/
http://www.bestfootforward.com/carbonlife.htm

Objectives

- Compares lifestyles of today with those of the past.
- Reads and understands informational text about the short- and long-term consequences of our lifestyle on the environment.

Curriculum links

Country	Subject	Level	Objectives
England	Literacy	Year 5	• Use evidence from a text to explain events or ideas.
		Year 6	• Understand underlying themes, causes and points of view.
Northern Ireland	Language and literacy	KS 2	• Engage in a range of reading activities.
Republic of Ireland	English	5th/6th Class	• Explore non-fiction texts and use comprehension skills.
Scotland	English	Level D	• Complete practical reading tasks.
Wales	English	KS 2	• Read for information.

Lifestyle and the environment

There is evidence to suggest that dinosaurs ruled the world until a huge asteroid collided with the earth about 65 million years ago, causing a mass extinction. With the rapid growth in human population from 1 billion people 200 years ago to over 6 billion people in the world today, we are now experiencing another 'extinction spasm'. However, this time it appears to be worse than ever before. But just how is this happening?

The answer is environmental problems caused by humans.

These include:

- Habitat destruction
- The over-taking of some animals for food and other products
- Air pollution, water pollution and soil degradation
- Potential global warming, which could produce the greatest extinction loss ever

What's interesting is that these environmental problems have not just been the result of increased population. They are also the result of the way in which many people live now compared with 200 years ago.

Imagine you were born in the year 1800. There are no cars, no electricity, no big factories, no large fishing industries, no large farms with farm machinery and no shopping centres. There is little machinery, so everything has to be done virtually by hand—people have their own vegetable gardens and farm animals and make their own clothes.

Now think about what we are doing today, 200 years later. We have advanced high-powered machinery, factories and electricity, huge farms and grazing lands, planes and automobiles and technology that allows people to extract huge numbers of fish from the oceans. And we want more than ever before—big houses, fast cars, fast food, the latest fashion, the best toys and the most up-to-date technology. It takes a lot of energy, minerals and natural supplies to make all these goods.

Our current lifestyle is a major cause of environmental problems—we are taking too much from the Earth and, when we do give something back, it's often pollution. Is it possible to live a happy life without destroying the earth? What changes can be made to fix the problems? What changes can *you* make?

Answers

1. (a) and (c)

T	D	E	S	T	R	U	C	T	I	O	N	A
R	E	X	P	A	N	S	I	O	N	O	H
G	N	X	G	O	S	N	P	M	P	N	I	T
D	O	T	I	R	T	S	A	E	O	G	T	E
E	S	I	N	O	A	L	S	L	L	T	A	C
A	A	N	D	R	R	D	M	E	L	H	L	H
D	U	C	U	K	P	F	A	Y	U	X	U	N
I	R	T	S	E	Q	D	A	I	T	K	P	O
O	S	I	I	Q	D	R	I	R	B	O	L
R	D	O	R	U	S	W	L	O	O	P	O
E	M	N	J	U	Z	F	C	N	G	N	G
T	J	V	E	M	A	C	H	I	N	E	R	Y
S	C	P	F	E	I	R	O	T	C	A	F	I
A	S	E	R	T	N	E	C	Y	U	O	B

(b) (i) spasm – sudden convulsive movement
 (ii) degrade – reduce to a lower rank
 (iii) expansion – increase in amount of territory

(c) (1) cars (2) factories (3) industries
 (4) machinery (5) centres (6) electricity

2. Possible answers:
 (a) Habitat destruction; the over-taking of some animals for food and other products; air pollution, water pollution and soil degradation; potential global warming.
 (b) An 'extinction spasm' refers to an event which results in mass extinction.
 (c) Humans now consume huge quantities of natural resources, produce huge quantities of pollution and cause mass destruction to natural environments to meet consumer needs.
 (d) Humans replace natural resources with pollutant by-products.

Objectives

- Identifies and understands the meaning of new words.
- Extracts relevant information about how our lifestyle affects the environment.

Curriculum links

Country	Subject	Level	Objectives
England	Literacy	Year 5	• Spell words and group words according to their meanings.
		Year 6	• Spell familiar words correctly and employ strategies to spell difficult words.
Northern Ireland	Language and literacy	KS 2	• Acquire and develop a vocabulary.
Republic of Ireland	English	5th/6th Class	• Extend and develop vocabulary and spelling.
Scotland	English	Level D/E	• Know specialist vocabulary from different curricular areas.
Wales	English	KS 2	• Use their knowledge gained from reading to develop their vocabulary.

4   The environment   www.prim-ed.com   Prim-Ed Publishing

Lifestyle and the environment

1. Complete these activities.

    (a) Find each new word in the puzzle.

    New words
    - dinosaurs
    - extinction
    - population
    - destruction
    - technology
    - asteroid
    - expansion
    - spasm
    - degradation
    - pollution

T	D	E	S	T	R	U	C	T	I	O	N	A
R	I	E	X	P	A	N	S	I	O	N	O	H
G	N	X	G	O	S	N	P	M	P	N	I	T
D	O	T	I	R	T	S	A	E	O	G	T	E
E	S	I	N	O	A	L	S	L	L	T	A	C
A	A	N	D	R	R	D	M	E	L	H	L	H
D	U	C	U	K	P	F	A	C	U	X	U	N
I	R	T	S	E	Q	D	A	T	T	K	P	O
O	S	I	T	Q	D	R	I	R	I	B	O	L
R	D	O	R	U	S	W	L	I	O	O	P	O
E	M	N	I	J	U	Z	F	C	N	G	N	G
T	J	V	E	M	A	C	H	I	N	E	R	Y
S	C	P	S	E	I	R	O	T	C	A	F	I
A	S	E	R	T	N	E	C	Y	Y	U	O	B

    (b) Write meanings for these words. Use a dictionary to help you.

    (i) spasm _____

    (ii) degrade _____

    (iii) expansion _____

    (c) There are six extra words hidden in the puzzle which describe living in the 1800s. Complete the passage by finding the missing words.

    In the 1800s there were no

    c_____(1), no big

    f_____(2), no large fishing

    i_____(3), no large farms

    with m_____(4), no

    shopping c_____(5)

    and there was no e_____(6).

2. Answer these questions.

    (a) List two environmental problems caused by humans.

    _____

    _____

    (b) What do you think is meant by an 'extinction spasm'?

    _____

    _____

    (c) Describe one way humans' use of the earth has changed over the past 200 years.

    _____

    _____

    _____

    (d) Humans are taking too many resources from the earth. What do they often put back in their place?

    _____

Teachers notes
Lifestyle and the environment

Answers

1. (a) food, shelter, water
   (b) Answers will vary
2. Answers will vary; lack of food, shelter and clothing —>removal of the basic needs of humans-> humans will not survive.
3. Answers will vary; disasters such as drought, flood or earthquakes, over-harvesting, land clearing and depletion of soil.

Additional activities

- In small groups, develop a 'top 10' list of the world's biggest environmental mistakes. Share with the class and suggest how the damage caused might be reversed.
- Debate what may have caused the extinction of dinosaurs and whether human activity could have the same result.
- Research the causes of famine in third world countries and the work which is being done by welfare organisations such as World Vision to help them.

Lesson outline

- Discuss briefly theories the pupils know for explaining the extinction of dinosaurs. Determine whether, based on these theories, humans may be in danger of extinction in the future.
- Read together the introductory passage at the top of the pupil worksheet. Discuss how a 'man-made' extinction spasm is different from an asteroid hitting the earth.
- Give the pupils time to write a list of requirements living things need to survive to complete Question 1(a). Have the pupils share their lists with the class and add to their own lists if necessary.
- Briefly discuss what humans are doing which threatens the basic needs of living things. Have the pupils use information from the class discussion to assist them in completing Question 1(b), referring specifically to human needs.
- Read the first group of italicized sentences on the pupil worksheet which follow. Have the pupils imagine a group of 75 000 objects to demonstrate the enormity of the problem. Have the pupils make general estimates of how many years they think we could continue losing species at this rate until there is no life left on earth.
- Discuss whether or not humans could survive without any other living things. Give the pupils time to complete Question 2.
- Read together the second group of italicized sentences which follow on the pupil worksheet. Using a globe or a world map, identify some places in the world where people are suffering from starvation. Encourage the pupils to suggest other reasons apart from war which may lead to famine. Have the pupils use the information from the discussion to complete Question 3.

Objective

- Identifies what living things need to survive and how human behaviour is destroying these requirements.

Curriculum links

Country	Subject	Level	Objectives
England	Geography	KS 2	Recognise how people can damage the environment and how decisions about environments affect the future quality of people's lives.
Northern Ireland	Geography	KS 2	Know some of the ways in which people affect the environment.
Republic of Ireland	Science/ Geography	5th/6th Class	Recognise human activities which may have adverse effects on environments and appreciate the need to conserve the Earth's resources.
Scotland	Science	Level D	Explain how responses to changes in the environment can be protected and give examples.
Wales	Geography	KS 2	Identify ways in which people affect the environment.

Lifestyle and the environment

This is the life ... or is it?

An extinction spasm is an event which leads to the extinction of a vast number of species—perhaps including people. Evidence suggests that a huge asteroid hit the Earth some 65 000 000 years ago, causing a massive cloud of dust which hovered in the atmosphere, preventing light from the sun reaching the Earth. This lasted long enough for plants to die. When the plants died, the animals which used them for food and shelter also died—including the dinosaurs.

We have no control over asteroids hitting the Earth. However, some scientists believe we are now beginning to experience a 'man-made extinction spasm'.

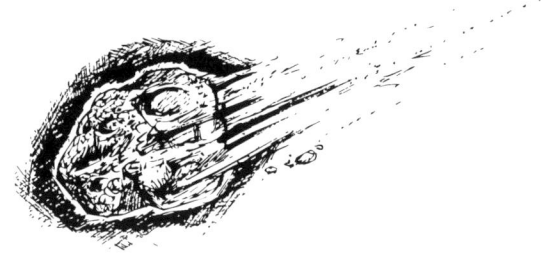

Discuss and take notes

1. (a) What do living things need to survive?

   (b) What are humans doing to destroy the things we need to survive?

The majority of the damage caused by humans has occurred over the past 200 years. Now, up to 75 000 species may become extinct every year.

2. How will the extinction of animals and plants affect humans?

In parts of the world, people are starving. Famine can be caused when war prevents food from being delivered to communities or prevents farms from operating successfully.

3. Suggest other reasons why famine might occur.

Teachers notes
Lifestyle and the environment

Lesson outline

- Provide stimulus pictures of machinery and living conditions from previous generations, or read an extract from an historical novel to demonstrate the contrast in lifestyle to today. Encourage the pupils to share stories they may have heard from their grandparents about life in the 'olden days'. Informally compare the resources which were consumed then to those consumed today.

- Read together the introductory passage at the top of the pupil worksheet. Encourage the pupils to compare their lifestyle to that of their parents at the same age. Discuss whether their lifestyle is an improvement on how their parents lived.

- Read Question 1 including the categories listed in the table from (a) to (g). Allow the pupils to work in pairs to decide how each 'lifestyle choice' impacts on the environment and to tick the appropriate boxes.

- Have the pupils write explanations for how the items selected in the spotlight boxes affect the environment to complete Question 2. For example, how does the production of electricity 1 (b) affect natural resources?

- Hold a class vote to determine whether or not the pupils would be willing to give up the things they are used to (cars, electricity, fast food etc.). Based on the vote, discuss whether or not people today would ever be likely to revert to the way people lived 200 years ago. Have the pupils complete Question 3.

- Encourage the pupils to suggest a compromise, where we are not required to give up the lifestyle we enjoy, but can also sustain our environment. Have the pupils take notes from the class discussion and write a list of ideas for reducing the impact we are having on our environment.

Answers

1. Teacher check
2. Spotlight (b) extraction of fossil fuels which are non-renewable.

   Spotlight (d) Trawling not only removes fish but disturbs and destroys their habitat.

   Spotlight (f) Fast food wrappers become litter. Cooking process produces pollutant by-products.
3. No
4. Teacher check

Additional activities

- In small groups, perform a case study on one of today's listed lifestyle choices. Invent, draft and annotate a new environmentally-friendly alternative to present to the class.

- Hold a 'back to 1800' day where no books or pencils (only chalk on boards), no electricity or running water and no canteen or pre-packed foods are used.

Objective

- Identify and discuss the impact changing technology has had on the environment.

Curriculum links

Country	Subject	Level	Objectives
England	Geography	KS 2	• Recognise human processes and explain how these can cause changes in environments.
Northern Ireland	Science and technology	KS 2	• Know about the use of energy and its effect on the environment.
Republic of Ireland	Science/ Geography	5th/6th Class	• Recognise human activities which may have adverse effects on environments and appreciate the need to conserve the Earth's resources.
Scotland	Society	Level D	• Describe effects of industrial processes on the environment.
Wales	Geography	KS 2	• Identify ways in which people affect the environment.

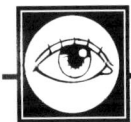

Lifestyle and the environment

Lifestyle comparison

The population of the world is increasing. Not only that, the lifestyles of many members of that population have changed dramatically to being fast-paced and reliant on technology. Most of this change has taken place in just the last 200 years.

1. Complete the grid below by ticking the appropriate boxes to compare the damage we cause to our environment today to that of 200 years ago.

	Lifestyle	Habitat destruction	Pollution	Overusing natural resources
(a)	Now – Fast cars			
	Then – No cars			
(b)	Now – Electricity			spotlight
	Then – No electrictiy			
(c)	Now – Large factories			
	Then – Small cottage industries			
(d)	Now – Technology for extracting huge numbers of fish	spotlight		
	Then – No large fishing industries			
(e)	Now – High-powered machinery			
	Then – Human or animal-powered machinery			
(f)	Now – Fast food		spotlight	
	Then – Home-grown food			
(g)	Now – Shopping centres with the latest fashion and toys			
	Then – Homemade toys and clothes			

2. Discuss each comparison and the impact change has had on the environment. Fill in the 'spotlight boxes' by describing how that destruction occurs.

3. Do you think it is likely that people will revert to the way people lived 200 years ago? **Yes** **No**

4. Compile a class list of ideas for reducing the impact we are having on our environment.

Teachers notes
Smart resources

Background information

Resources are likened to natural capital—a source of wealth used to support life. They provide not only the needs required by humans, but just as importantly, for all other animals and plants on the earth. Fossil fuels and nuclear energy are finite and are examples of non-renewable resources. Air, water, forests, fisheries and products of agriculture are examples of renewable resources. These living products of the world require no human effort to be brought back to the original state after having been used. They continue to exist and reappear due to the processes of natural nutrients cycling through the environment.

Renewable resources still have the potential to be damaged or even destroyed. Species extinction results in the loss of a renewable resource. Scientists have developed and are currently exploring many alternatives to non-renewable resources, particularly in the area of renewable energy. But without the proper management of resources (i.e. allowing the loss of biodiversity), ecosystems can lose balance and are unable to maintain their quality.

This has serious ramifications for society and, unfortunately, detrimental effects have already resulted from the loss of natural capital we have recently experienced during the industrial revolution. A shift to clean renewable energy is an example of how to correctly manage natural resources to ensure the ongoing health of the planet and, in turn, its viability for future generations.

Discussion points

- What is meant by 'by-product'?
- Why do you think renewable energy sources were not used in the first place?
- What problems may be encountered in changing from non-renewable to renewable energy sources?

Websites

http://www.populationinstitute.org/

http://www.bestfootforward.com/carbonlife.htm

Objective

- Reads and understands informational text about renewable and non-renewable resources.

Curriculum links

Country	Subject	Level	Objectives
England	Literacy	Year 5	• Use evidence from a text to explain events or ideas.
		Year 6	• Understand underlying themes, causes and points of view.
Northern Ireland	Language and literacy	KS 2	• Engage in a range of reading activities.
Republic of Ireland	English	5th/6th Class	• Explore non-fiction texts and use comprehension skills.
Scotland	English	Level D	• Complete practical reading tasks.
Wales	English	KS 2	• Read for information.

Smart resources

A resource is defined as anything obtained from the living or non-living environment to meet human needs and wants. Some resources run out—like coal which is mined from beneath the earth and used to make electricity. These resources are called non-renewable resources. Others, like fish caught from the oceans and eaten for food, should never run out because they keep reproducing. These are called renewable resources and they are definitely the 'smart alternative'. 'Smart' because, if carefully managed, these resources can be sustained forever.

We have to start thinking about alternatives for those non-renewable resources which we are currently taking from our environment before they run out. For example, coal is burned to make electricity. But once it is burned it is gone forever as a resource, while producing a lot of pollution as a by-product. One day all the coal in the world will be gone. So scientists have discovered other ways to make electricity, including:

- wind power
- solar power
- moving water power
- geothermal power (heat from below the earth's surface).

These are all renewable resources because they do not run out—they are smart alternatives to using resources that will run out. Plus there are no nasty pollution by-products like there are in burning coal. So the more we use these alternative 'smart' electricity sources and the sooner we stop using resources like coal, the better.

Teachers notes
Smart resources

Answers

1. (a) and (c)

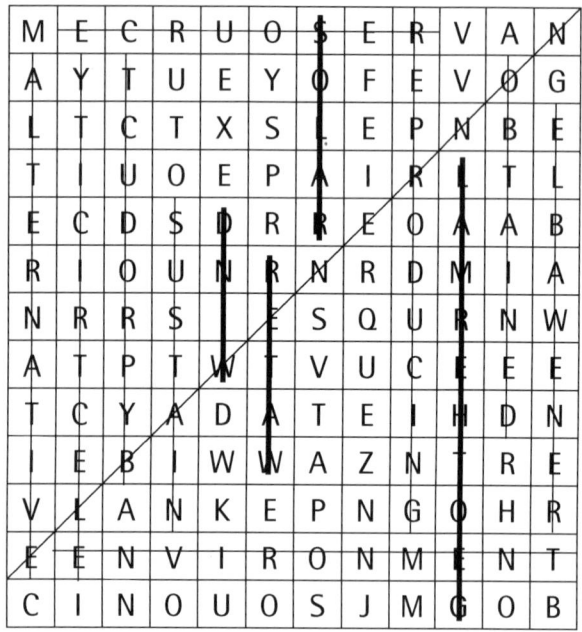

(b) (i) Resource—means of supplying what is needed, stock that can be drawn on.

(ii) Alternative—one of two or more possibilities

(iii) Sustain—keep going continually

(c) (i) wind (ii) solar (iii) water (iv) geothermal

2. (a) A resource is anything obtained from the living or non-living environment to meet human needs and wants.

(b) (i) Non-renewable resources

(ii) Renewable resources

(c) A by-product is any unwanted element produced in the processes of making a product.

(d) Alternative electricity sources are 'smart' because they will not run out and they do not produce pollutant by-products.

Objectives

- Identifies and understands the meaning of new words.
- Extracts relevant information about renewable and non-renewable resources.

Curriculum links

Country	Subject	Level	Objectives
England	Literacy	Year 5	• Spell words and group words according to their meanings.
		Year 6	• Spell familiar words correctly and employ strategies to spell difficult words.
Northern Ireland	Language and literacy	KS 2	• Acquire and develop a vocabulary.
Republic of Ireland	English	5th/6th Class	• Extend and develop vocabulary and spelling.
Scotland	English	Level D/E	• Know specialist vocabulary from different curricular areas.
Wales	English	KS 2	• Use their knowledge gained from reading to develop their vocabulary.

12   The environment   www.prim-ed.com   Prim-Ed Publishing

Smart resources

1. Complete these activities.

   (a) Find each new word in the puzzle.

   New words
   - resource
   - environment
   - renewable
   - alternative
   - by-product
   - obtained
   - non-renewable
   - reproducing
   - sustain
   - electricity

M	E	C	R	U	O	S	E	R	V	A	N
A	Y	T	U	E	Y	O	F	E	V	O	G
L	T	C	T	X	S	L	E	P	N	B	E
T	I	U	O	E	P	A	I	R	L	T	L
E	C	D	S	D	R	R	E	O	A	A	B
R	I	O	U	N	R	N	R	D	M	I	A
N	R	R	S	I	E	S	Q	U	R	N	W
A	T	P	T	W	T	V	U	C	E	E	E
T	C	Y	A	D	A	T	E	I	H	D	N
I	E	B	I	W	W	A	Z	N	T	R	E
V	L	A	N	K	E	P	N	G	O	H	R
E	E	N	V	I	R	O	N	M	E	N	T
C	I	N	O	U	O	S	J	M	G	O	B

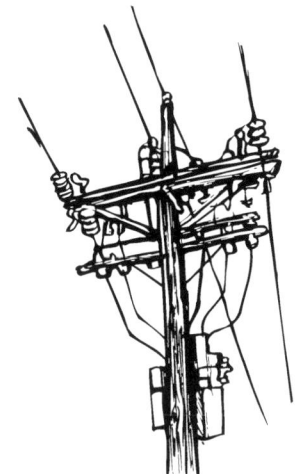

   (b) Write meanings for these words. Use a dictionary to help you.

   (i) resource _____

   (ii) alternative _____

   (iii) sustain _____

   (c) There are four extra words hidden in the puzzle which are renewable electricity sources. Can you find them?

   (i)   w_____ power
   (ii) s_____ power
   (iii) moving w_____ power
   (iv) g_____ power

2. Answer these questions.

   (a) What is a resource?
   _____
   _____
   _____

   (b) (i) What are the resources that run out called?
   _____

   (ii) What are the resources that do not run out called?
   _____

   (c) Describe what you think is meant by the term 'by-product'.
   _____
   _____
   _____

   (d) Why are the alternative electricity sources 'smart'?
   _____
   _____
   _____

Teachers notes
Smart resources

Answers

1. Teacher check
2. (a) Teacher check
   (b) Answers will vary
3. Answers will vary

Additional activities

- Investigate how a full-scale turbine works in a hydro-electric plant. Find out how electricity is produced from reservoir water at Ffestiniog power station in Wales.
- As a whole class, brainstorm a list of actual and potential uses for energy. Evaluate the necessity of each.

Lesson outline

- Review what is meant by a 'smart resource'. Have the pupils suggest some 'smart' energy sources. Encourage them to think how these resources are already being used to produce energy in the world today and, more specifically, in their country or city. Make reference to existing hydro-electric power stations such as the Ffestiniog and Dinorwig power stations in Wales and to the 'wind farms' at Orkney and Shetland in Scotland.

- Read together the introductory passage at the top of the pupil activity page. If possible, provide pictures or models of turbines for the pupils to see or handle. Direct the pupils to the explanation of how turbines work on the pupil activity page.

- Allow the pupils to work independently or with a partner to design and make their own turbine using simple materials. Give the pupils ample opportunity to 'test' the efficiency of their turbines. If time permits, allow the pupils to view the turbines made by other pupils in the class and compare why some work better than others. Make comparisons based on the materials used, the size of the turbine and any other criteria deemed relevant by the pupils.

- Have the pupils evaluate their own invention on the scale in Question 2 (a) and to suggest how their turbine could have been improved for a better result to complete 2 (b).

- Based on the pupils' own invention and what they observed about the inventions of their peers, have them suggest the types of materials and resources which would be needed for their invention to work most efficiently on a large scale. Encourage the pupils to share their thoughts with the class and 'inspire' one another as they complete Question 3.

Objectives

- Understands that a natural resource such as water or wind can be used to produce energy.
- Designs and evaluates the effectiveness of a simple turbine.

Curriculum links

Country	Subject	Level	Objectives
England	Design and technology	KS 2	• Investigate products, thinking about how they work and are used and complete design and make assignments.
Northern Ireland	Science and technology	KS 2	• Design and make a model that uses a renewable energy source.
Republic of Ireland	Science	5th/6th Class	• Explore objects, how they work and how they could be made.
Scotland	Technology	Level D	• Use ideas to represent a solution to a practical task.
Wales	Design and technology	KS 2	• Evaluate, design and make products.

Smart resources

Resources with a future

Not only can water be used to drink, to water and grow our plants and to keep us clean, it can also be used to produce energy. Energy causes things to move. Water can be used in many ways to cause things to move. In fact, if a turbine can be made to spin fast enough, electricity can be produced.

1. Create your own turbine and invent a way to use water to make it spin as fast as possible.

   Draw and label a diagram of your invention.

   A turbine is a cylinder with protruding paddles around it which can be filled with water or wind to turn it. A windmill is a simple turbine. When the turbine spins very quickly, it can generate enough energy to make electricity.

2. Evaluation

   (a) How did your invention work?

   excellent   **pretty good**   **okay**   **not well**   **fell apart**

   (b) What could you do to improve your invention? _____
   _____
   _____

3. For your invention to work on a large scale, what resources would you need?

Teachers notes
Smart resources

Lesson outline

- Clarify what is meant by non-renewable and renewable resources by reading the introductory sentences at the top of the pupil activity page. Read together the things listed in the 'sun' shape.

- Give the pupils time to classify each of the things listed in the sun shape as renewable or non-renewable in the table provided to complete Question 1. Allow the pupils to discuss their choices with their peers or a designated partner if required.

- Instruct the pupils to complete Question 2 independently to give their own reason for why non-renewable resources shouldn't all be used. Encourage the pupils to share and justify their reasoning to the class.

- Discuss why renewable resources aren't being readily used. Consider issues such as the cost of setting up new infrastructure, the loss of jobs in mining industries and the subsequent loss of wealth for those who have invested in such enterprises. Consider the power held by people in such positions and the level of control they may have over industry and development. Consider also the technology required to be able to use renewable energy efficiently and whether or not there are people developing this kind of technology.

- Allow the pupils to write their own opinion why they think non-renewable resources are still being used to complete Question 3.

- Divide the class into small groups to answer Question 4. Have them discuss briefly what they think their household would be like if there were no more non-renewable resources to be used. Encourage the pupils to then write a description of their lifestyle. If time permits, allow the groups to draw a picture annotating things which would be different in their lifestyle. Display the drawings for the class to see or have the pupils hold them in front of the class and explain their predictions.

Answers

1. Renewable—people, wind, sheep, wheat, fish, bananas, water, sun, timber, cattle

   Non-renewable—oil, mountains, mineral sands, natural gas, bauxite, lead, gold, coal

2. We should not use all the non-renewable resources because when they are used they cannot be replaced.

3. Answers will vary; Renewable resources aren't being used as much as non-renewable resources because it is expensive to set up an infrastructure for using renewable resources.

4. Answers will vary.

Additional activities

- Develop a class list of renewable resources. Identify those which could be destroyed by current human behaviour.

- Make signs or leaflets giving suggestions as to what people can do to help protect and make the most of the renewable resources we have.

Objectives

- Identifies renewable and non-renewable resources.
- Realises the consequences of overusing non-renewable resources.

Curriculum links

Country	Subject	Level	Objectives
England	Geography	KS 2	• Recognise how and why people may seek to manage environments sustainably.
Northern Ireland	Geography	KS 2	• Investigate the use of natural resources in the environment and the importance of conserving them.
Republic of Ireland	Geography/ Science	5th/6th Class	• Become aware of the Earth's renewable and non-renewable resources and come to appreciate the need to conserve the Earth's resources.
Scotland	Science	Level E	• Explain the difference between renewable and non-renewable energy resources.
Wales	Geography	KS 2	• Investigate ways in which people attempt to look after the present and safeguard the future environment.

Smart resources

What happens in 50 years?

Resources which can run out are called non-renewable resources. Resources which cannot run out or that can reproduce are called renewable resources.

1. List each of the resources in the sun as renewable or non-renewable.

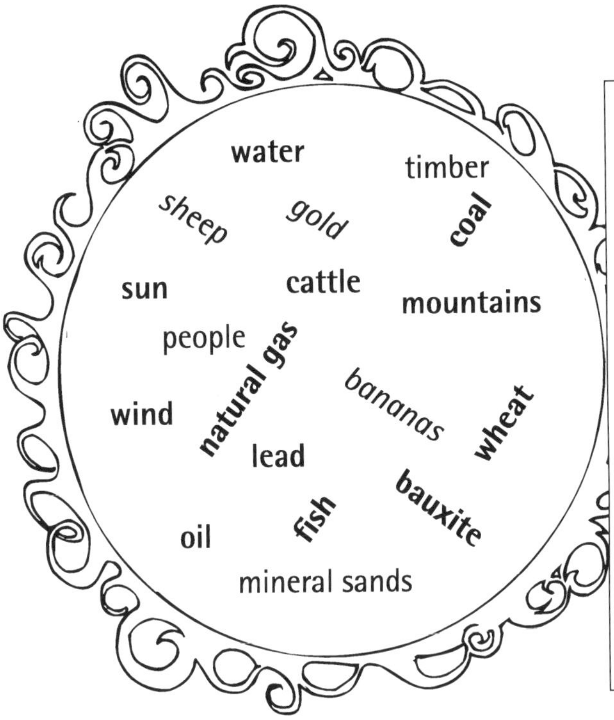

Resources in the sun: water, timber, sheep, gold, coal, sun, cattle, mountains, people, natural gas, bananas, wheat, wind, lead, fish, bauxite, oil, mineral sands

renewable	non-renewable

2. Why shouldn't we use all the non-renewable resources?

_____

3. Why do you think renewable resources aren't being used as much as non-renewable resources?

_____

Discuss

4. (a) What will your household be like in 50 years, if our non-renewable resources run out?

_____

(b) Write a description of what you imagine your lifestyle might be like in that case.

_____

Prim-Ed Publishing   www.prim-ed.com   **The environment**   17

Teachers notes
Can we run out of fish?

Background information

Fish are an enormously important renewable natural resource, providing the principal source of protein for approximately 1 billion people. Fifty per cent of the world's population lives within 100 kilometres of the coast. For this reason the oceans play a significant role in the lives of most people, providing food, income through fisheries and associated industries, and recreation.

The oceans have long been seen as an endless supply of fish and other products. Covering 71% of the planet and containing 80% of the world's life forms, surely the chances of depleting resources must be impossible. But, unfortunately, the impossible has happened.

Currently, 15 out of the world's 17 largest fisheries are either over-fished or in trouble. In fact, nearly 70% of our major marine fish stocks are over-fished or at their biological limit. Of major continuing concern is the huge number of marine creatures that are killed for nothing—as the by-catch of non-target species. This can be up to 50% of the catch and not only includes other fish species, but crustaceans, molluscs, birds and even mammals such as dolphins.

The major causes for the decline include over-harvesting and the destruction and pollution of fish breeding grounds. Correct management of this natural resource obviously includes the retention of clean breeding grounds, but the control of over-harvesting is a complex problem. Most people in the fishing industry want a sustainable industry and are striving towards solutions which include international fishing treaties/agreements on quantities, times when fishing is permitted (allowing for regeneration of stocks) and regulating types of machinery used (e.g. moves to reduce by-product catch and decrease the destruction of ocean beds by reducing/eliminating trawling).

Fortunately, all legislative changes which regulate fisheries around the world are moving towards solutions in sustainability, and thereby protecting not only this wonderful natural resource but also the livelihood of people in the industry.

Discussion points

- Explain what is meant by over-harvesting and habitat destruction. Are these problems shared by other renewable resources? Give examples.
- What do you think happens to fishing by-product?
- Suggest how the fishing industry could endeavour to manage its resources.

Websites

http://www.seaweb.org/home.php
http://www.abc.net.au/oceans/alive.htm
http://www.aquanet.com/

Objective

- Reads and understands informational text about sustaining renewable resources.

Curriculum links

Country	Subject	Level	Objectives
England	Literacy	Year 5	• Use evidence from a text to explain events or ideas.
		Year 6	• Understand underlying themes, causes and points of view.
Northern Ireland	Language and literacy	KS 2	• Engage in a range of reading activities.
Republic of Ireland	English	5th/6th Class	• Explore non-fiction texts and use comprehension skills.
Scotland	English	Level D	• Complete practical reading tasks.
Wales	English	KS 2	• Read for information.

Can we run out of fish?

Fish provide food and income for people in many countries around the world. Because fish reproduce rapidly and the oceans are so large, fish are a wonderful renewable resource.

But, is it possible that a renewable resource could be damaged so badly that it runs out? The answer is yes, and that is exactly what is happening with fish. There is a decline of about one-third of the catch of major commercial fish. This is the result of two main problems:

1. Over-harvesting—when more fish are taken than can be reproduced.

2. Habitat destruction and pollution of coastal wetlands, sea grasses and coral reefs which provide breeding grounds for about two-thirds of the world's fish.

So when we are thinking about taking resources from the environment to meet our needs, we need to be careful about what we are doing. We have to consider the correct management of renewable resources to ensure that we do not damage that resource in some way. This should never be the case with things like solar power (because the sun doesn't run out) and wind power (because there will always be wind), but it can affect other renewable resources such as timber needed to build houses.

Certainly the poor management of fish harvesting around the world is a good example of why we must quickly improve the way we look after our renewable resources. It doesn't just mean reducing the amount of fish we catch, but also the way we treat the whole of the Earth's environment.

Prim-Ed Publishing   www.prim-ed.com   **The environment**   19

Teachers notes
Can we run out of fish?

Answers

1. (a) and (c)

S	C	A	V	L	H	E	U	Y	K	D
N	O	I	R	H	A	B	I	T	A	T
T	U	L	F	M	R	R	N	Q	L	M
E	N	E	A	S	V	E	C	U	A	A
D	T	N	Z	R	E	E	O	X	I	N
E	R	I	T	E	S	D	M	T	C	A
G	I	L	S	D	T	I	E	N	R	G
A	E	C	G	I	I	N	H	P	E	E
M	S	E	N	V	N	G	O	W	M	M
A	I	D	N	O	G	A	J	C	M	E
D	E	S	T	R	U	C	T	I	O	N
B	O	R	A	P	I	D	L	Y	C	T

(b) (i) decline—fall, gradual loss
 (ii) commercial—for financial return rather than artistry
 (iii) harvest—reaping or gathering in of grain or other product

(c) (i) over-harvesting   (ii) habitat destruction

2. (a) There has been a decline of about one-third of the catch of major commercial fish.

(b) Answers will vary

(c) Fish and timber are potentially renewable resources—they will only be renewable if carefully monitored. The sun and the wind are renewable and cannot be affected by the activities of humans.

(d) Answers will vary

Objectives

- Identifies and understands the meaning of new words.
- Extracts relevant information about sustaining renewable resources.

Curriculum links

Country	Subject	Level	Objectives
England	Literacy	Year 5	• Spell words and group words according to their meanings.
		Year 6	• Spell familiar words correctly and employ strategies to spell difficult words.
Northern Ireland	Language and literacy	KS 2	• Acquire and develop a vocabulary.
Republic of Ireland	English	5th/6th Class	• Extend and develop vocabulary and spelling.
Scotland	English	Level D/E	• Know specialist vocabulary from different curricular areas.
Wales	English	KS 2	• Use their knowledge gained from reading to develop their vocabulary.

Can we run out of fish?

1. **Complete these activities.**

   (a) Find each new word in the puzzle.

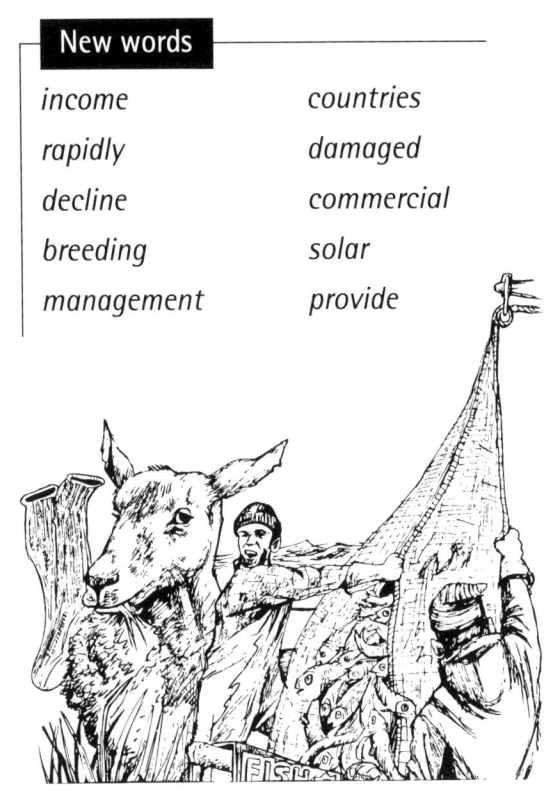

   New words
   - income
   - rapidly
   - decline
   - breeding
   - management
   - countries
   - damaged
   - commercial
   - solar
   - provide

S	C	A	V	L	H	E	U	Y	K	D
N	O	I	R	H	A	B	I	T	A	T
T	U	L	F	M	R	R	N	Q	L	M
E	N	E	A	S	V	E	C	U	A	A
D	T	N	Z	R	E	E	O	X	I	N
E	R	I	T	E	S	D	M	T	C	A
G	I	L	S	D	T	I	E	N	R	G
A	E	C	G	I	I	N	H	P	E	E
M	S	E	N	V	N	G	O	W	M	M
A	I	D	N	O	G	A	J	C	M	E
D	E	S	T	R	U	C	T	I	O	N
B	O	R	A	P	I	D	L	Y	C	T

   (b) Write meanings for these words. Use a dictionary to help you.

   (i) decline _____

   (ii) commercial _____

   (iii) harvest _____

   (c) There are three extra words hidden in the puzzle which are reasons why there has been a decline in the number of fish in our oceans. Can you find them?

   (i) over-_____
   (ii) h_____
   (iii) d_____

2. **Answer these questions.**

   (a) How much of a decline in the catch of major commercial fish has there been?
   _____
   _____

   (b) Name another renewable resource which may be threatened.
   _____

   (c) How are the renewable resources of the sun and wind different from the renewable resources of fish and timber?
   _____
   _____
   _____
   _____

   (d) How do you think the decline in fish could be reversed?
   _____
   _____
   _____

Teachers notes
Can we run out of fish?

Answers

1. Sharks—decrease due to lack of seals and fish to eat; seals—decrease due to lack of squid and fish to eat; crabs—increase initially due to decrease in fish eating them and then decrease due to lack of food; krill would increase initially due to lack of natural predators; squid would increase initially due to increase in krill and decrease in seals.
2. Answers will vary.

Additional activities

- Have a seafood sampling luncheon. Investigate why seafood is a healthy food for humans. (CAUTION: Some people have acute allergic reactions to seafood.)
- Investigate causes other than over-harvesting and habitat destruction to explain the decline in fish. Have the pupils write an argument encouraging the benefits of managing fish as a resource.

Lesson outline

- Encourage the pupils to share 'fish' experiences; for example, learning how to fish and fishing stories, pet fish and fish eating experiences. Ask the pupils whether or not they think it would matter if fish didn't exist. Ask the pupils to justify their stance.

- Read together the introductory passage at the top of the pupil activity page. Review how a food chain works by drawing a simple example for the pupils to view. A good example would be krill > squid > seal > shark. Describe the role each element in the food chain plays and the effect each has on the other.

- Introduce the concept of a food 'web' which is more complicated as there are more interacting elements. Direct the pupils to the food web on the pupil activity page. Have the pupils discuss with a partner or in a small group the effect each element would have on the other and the consequences of fish not existing.

- Have the pupils write a simple sentence to describe what would happen to each element on the food web if fish were removed. Encourage the pupils to consider an initial change and a long-term change for each.

- Read together the passage on the pupil page about sharks. Encourage the pupils to share their experiences with sharks or shark stories they may have heard or read about. Discuss whether the pupils believe sharks should be protected.

- Introduce the hypothetical discussion in Question two. Allow the pupils time to write two or three sentences in support of their argument for or against the protection of Great White sharks.

Objectives

- Understands the importance of fish in our diet.
- Explains what would happen to elements in an aquatic food web if fish were eliminated.

Curriculum links

Country	Subject	Level	Objectives
England	Science	KS 2	• Use food chains to show feeding relationships in a habitat.
Northern Ireland	Geography	KS 2	• Know about the use of natural resources in the environment and the importance of conserving them.
Republic of Ireland	Science	5th/6th Class	• Identify the interrelationships between animals in habitats; e.g. food chains and food webs.
Scotland	Science	Level E	• Construct and interpret simple food webs and make predictions of the consequences of change.
Wales	Science	KS 2	• Know that food chains show feeding relationships in an ecosystem.

Can we run out of fish?

Why we need fish

Imagine a world without fish. How would it affect you? From a health point of view, fish are an excellent food. They contain special oils, such as omega 3, which are important for the health of humans.

Even if you do not eat fish, they are still important to humans and the health of the planet in other ways. When fish are removed from the ocean, it affects the way many other creatures live.

1. Look at this simplified food web. Explain what would happen to each element if the web were broken and there were no more fish.

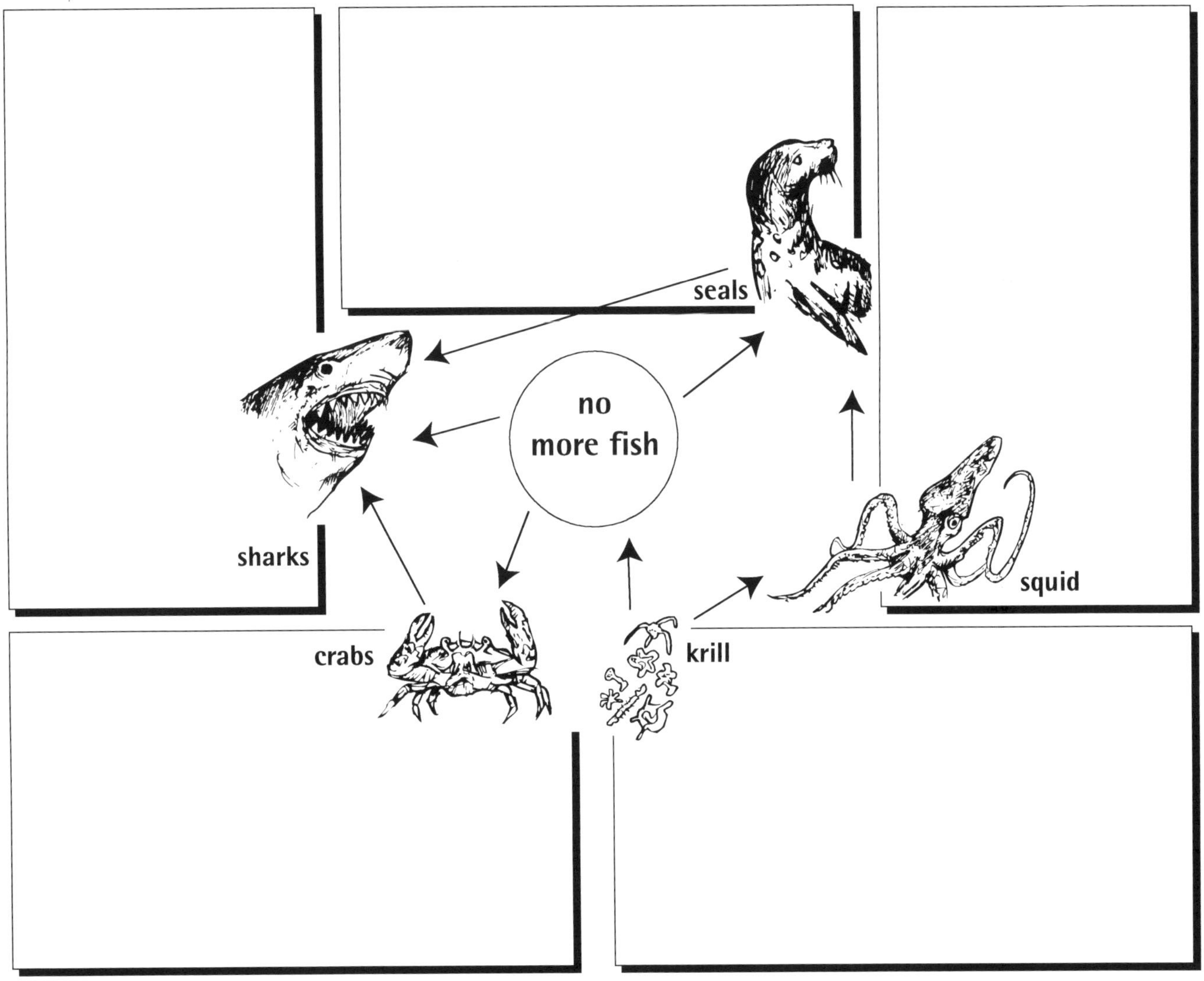

(Food web diagram with "no more fish" in the centre, connected to sharks, seals, squid, krill and crabs.)

Sharks are a threat to swimmers, surfers and divers. Often, we don't feel safe thinking that there may be sharks in the water. But, when sharks decrease in numbers, seals increase and eat all the fish we would normally catch and eat. This is what has happened in the oceans surrounding Australia. In fact, Great White sharks are now an endangered species.

Discussion

2. Imagine a shark has attacked and killed a swimmer at a beach. Should the shark be killed, even though it is endangered?

Teachers notes
Can we run out of fish?

Lesson outline

- Show the pupils a can of tuna with a dolphin safe logo. Ask the pupils how the tuna got into the can. Question the pupils as to how the anglers might have caught the tuna specifically and why the dolphin safe logo has been displayed.

- Read together the introductory paragraph at the top of the pupil activity page. Ask the pupils what might happen to anglers if fish ran out, to demonstrate the angler's need to protect their own industry rather than over-harvest. Question the pupils as to why anglers might be so determined not to kill other sea creatures.

- Direct the pupils to the three inventions illustrated in Question 1. Discuss how each works and read the explanation given in part (a). After discussion as to how each of the remaining inventions work, allow the pupils to complete Question 1.

- Have the pupils read the information describing shortfalls in the inventions shown. Allow the pupils to work in pairs to invent a device to catch sardines without catching sharks as outlined in Question 2.

- Allow the pupils time to draw and label a diagram of their device in the box provided. If the device is complicated it may be necessary for the pupils to draw their diagram on the reverse side of the page or on another sheet of paper.

- Give the pupils the opportunity to describe their device to the class, including how it operates, the materials used and any special features. Members of the class should be encouraged to evaluate the inventions and make constructive suggestions as to how an invention might be improved where appropriate.

Answers

1. (b) Anglers were finding turtles caught in their nets. 'TED' works by only allowing fish through a grid which is too narrow to allow turtles to pass.

   (c) Anglers were finding large sea creatures such as dolphins entangled in their nets. 'Pingers' work by emitting a signal which repels dolphins and other sea mammals.

2. Answers will vary

Additional activities

- Pupils bring in or identify products in the supermarket displaying a dolphin friendly symbol. Investigate what the symbol represents.

- Write a recipe using seafood. Create a class seafood cookbook of the pupils' suggestions.

Objective

- Explains how devices for catching specific fish have been developed so as not to catch sealife unnecessarily.

Curriculum links

Country	Subject	Level	Objectives
England	Geography	KS 2	• Recognise why people may seek to manage environments sustainably.
Northern Ireland	Geography	KS 2	• Investigate the use of natural resources in the environment and the importance of conserving them.
Republic of Ireland	Geography/Science	5th/6th Class	• Come to appreciate the need to conserve the Earth's resources.
Scotland	Society	Level D	• Describe some methods used and reasons for conserving major resources.
Wales	Geography	KS 2	• Investigate ways in which people attempt to look after the present and safeguard the future environment through sustainable development.

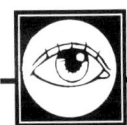

Can we run out of fish?

Good fishermen

Most anglers are going to great lengths to ensure that the fishing industry can be sustained and the fish don't run out. Scientists around the world are working hard to invent ways to catch the specific type and number of fish they want without catching other sea creatures which would otherwise die and be wasted. Look at these three great inventions currently being used in our fishing industry.

1. How do you think these inventions work? The first one has been described for you.

(a) Underwater setting for long line tuna fishing

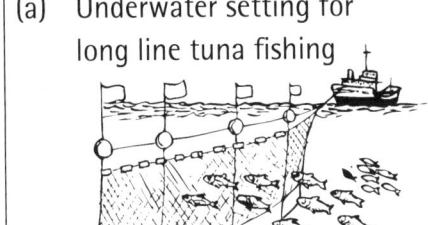

The anglers were finding albatrosses (large threatened seabirds) on their tuna hooks. Sometimes they were caught as the lines were cast, or before the bait had defrosted and was still floating on the surface. Scientists developed a way to cast the lines from underneath the boat and defrosted the bait so that it would not float to the surface.

(b) 'TED' (Turtle Excluding Device)

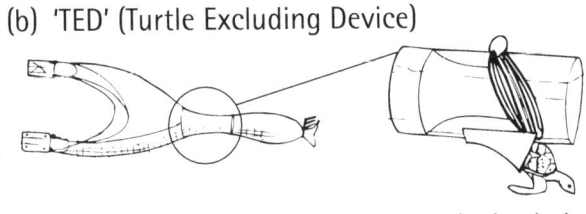

Anglers were finding turtles caught in their nets. 'TED' works by ...

(c) 'Pingers' attached to gill nets.

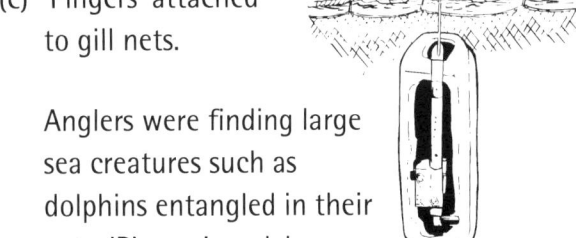

Anglers were finding large sea creatures such as dolphins entangled in their nets. 'Pingers' work by ...

These devices are still not perfect. Sometimes, sharks become entangled in the nets and die. Scientists are still working on ways to prevent this from happening.

2. Can you help the scientists? Can you invent a device to catch sardines without catching sharks and other large sea creatures? Draw and label your design in the box provided.

Teachers notes
A tree named Luna

Background information

An old-growth forest is where individual trees can be up to 1000 years old as in the case of Luna—a giant redwood tree in America. Giant redwood trees are the tallest trees in the world. The oldest exceeds 2000 years of age. Yet these trees are still being harvested for timber.

About 90% of all old-growth forests end up as paper and some of that pulp may sell for as little as the price of a pair of socks per tonne. Can you imagine trees of such grandeur being reduced to something almost valueless?

Old-growth forests are important not only for their intrinsic value, but also because it takes 50 to 100 years before a tree will develop hollows. Many wildlife species are dependent on hollows for shelter and breeding. Replacing old-growth forests with regeneration or plantation vegetation will not satisfy hollow-dependent species, and they simply die out from these areas.

What is particularly noteworthy about this true story of Julia and her tree named Luna is that young people can and do make a difference in the quest to 'save the planet'. Although Julia went to the absolute extreme, all people, young and old should contribute wherever they can to both reducing pollution and recycling.

Setting up the classroom (permanently) to encourage these ideals is a must if we wish to lead by example.

Discussion points

- What point was Julia trying to make by living in a tree? Do you think it was worth it?
- Are you an environmentally friendly consumer – why?

Websites

http://www.geocities.com/albioncircle/JuliaHill.html
http://www.nps.gov/archive/redw/trees.html
http://www.wilderness.org/

Objectives

- Reads and understands informational text about the importance of sustaining old-growth forests.
- Reads and understands informational text about ideas for recycling.

Curriculum links

Country	Subject	Level	Objectives
England	Literacy	Year 5	• Use evidence from a text to explain events or ideas.
		Year 6	• Understand underlying themes, causes and points of view.
Northern Ireland	Language and literacy	KS 2	• Engage in a range of reading activities.
Republic of Ireland	English	5th/6th Class	• Explore non-fiction texts and use comprehension skills.
Scotland	English	Level D	• Complete practical reading tasks.
Wales	English	KS 2	• Read for information.

A tree named Luna

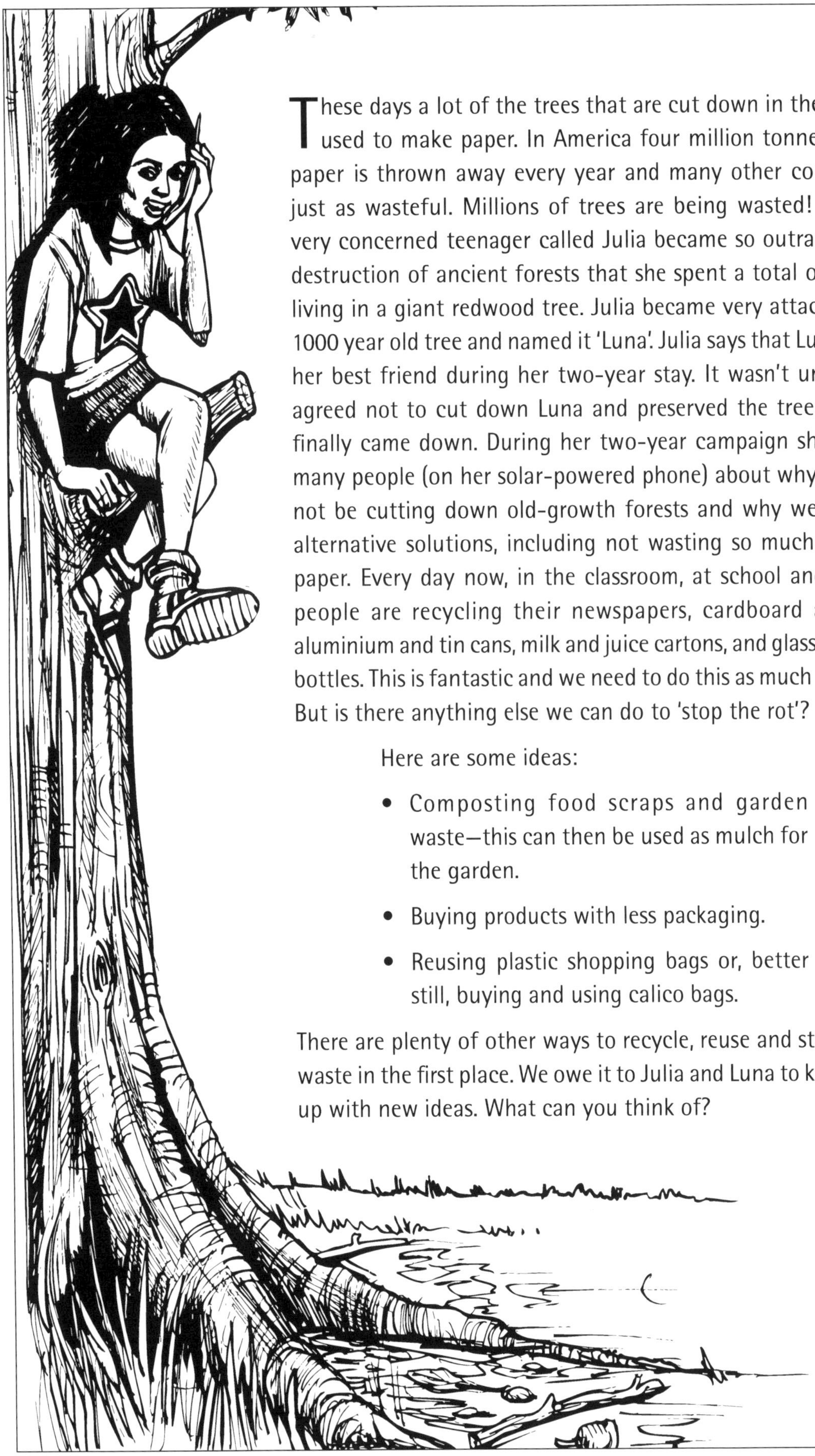

These days a lot of the trees that are cut down in the world are used to make paper. In America four million tonnes of office paper is thrown away every year and many other countries are just as wasteful. Millions of trees are being wasted! In 1998 a very concerned teenager called Julia became so outraged by the destruction of ancient forests that she spent a total of 738 days living in a giant redwood tree. Julia became very attached to her 1000 year old tree and named it 'Luna'. Julia says that Luna became her best friend during her two-year stay. It wasn't until loggers agreed not to cut down Luna and preserved the tree, that Julia finally came down. During her two-year campaign she spoke to many people (on her solar-powered phone) about why we should not be cutting down old-growth forests and why we must find alternative solutions, including not wasting so much wood and paper. Every day now, in the classroom, at school and at home, people are recycling their newspapers, cardboard and paper, aluminium and tin cans, milk and juice cartons, and glass and plastic bottles. This is fantastic and we need to do this as much as possible. But is there anything else we can do to 'stop the rot'?

Here are some ideas:

- Composting food scraps and garden waste—this can then be used as mulch for the garden.
- Buying products with less packaging.
- Reusing plastic shopping bags or, better still, buying and using calico bags.

There are plenty of other ways to recycle, reuse and stop creating waste in the first place. We owe it to Julia and Luna to keep coming up with new ideas. What can you think of?

Teachers notes
A tree named Luna

Answers

1. (a) and (c)

C	O	M	P	O	S	T	I	N	G
K	T	I	L	U	N	A	D	G	G
G	J	L	R	T	O	N	N	I	N
C	U	L	W	R	I	C	I	A	I
W	L	I	E	A	T	I	B	P	L
A	I	O	S	G	U	E	S	M	C
S	A	N	U	E	L	N	T	A	Y
T	I	F	M	E	D	O	T	L	C	C
E	D	P	R	E	S	E	R	V	E
D	A	Q	U	V	H	P	Y	E	R

(b) (i) outrage—cause to feel great resentment
    (ii) preserve—to keep undisturbed
    (iii) campaign—organised course of action
(c) Julia, Luna

2. (a) A lot of trees are cut down to make paper.
   (b) (i) Julia was outraged by the destruction of ancient forests.
       (ii) Julia spent 738 days living in a giant redwood tree.
   (c) Newspaper, cardboard, paper, aluminium cans, tin cans, milk cartons, juice cartons, glass, plastic bottles.
   (d) Answers will vary.

Objectives

- Identifies and understands the meaning of new words.
- Extracts relevant information about sustaining old-growth forests and recycling.

Curriculum links

Country	Subject	Level	Objectives
England	Literacy	Year 5	• Spell words and group words according to their meanings.
		Year 6	• Spell familiar words correctly and employ strategies to spell difficult words.
Northern Ireland	Language and literacy	KS 2	• Acquire and develop a vocabulary.
Republic of Ireland	English	5th/6th Class	• Extend and develop vocabulary and spelling.
Scotland	English	Level D/E	• Know specialist vocabulary from different curricular areas.
Wales	English	KS 2	• Use their knowledge gained from reading to develop their vocabulary.

A tree named Luna

1. Complete these activities.

    (a) Find each new word in the puzzle.

    New words

    million   wasted
    outraged   ancient
    preserve   campaign
    solution   recycling
    composting   reuse

    | C | O | M | P | O | S | T | I | N | G |
    | K | T | I | L | U | N | A | D | G | G |
    | G | J | L | R | T | O | N | N | I | N |
    | C | U | L | W | R | I | C | I | A | I |
    | W | L | I | E | A | T | I | B | P | L |
    | A | I | O | S | G | U | E | S | M | C |
    | S | A | N | U | E | L | N | T | A | Y |
    | T | F | M | E | D | O | T | L | C | C |
    | E | D | P | R | E | S | E | R | V | E |
    | D | A | Q | U | V | H | P | Y | E | R |

    (b) Write meanings for these words. Use a dictionary to help you.

    (i) outrage _____

    (ii) preserve _____

    (iii) campaign _____

    (c) There are two extra words hidden in the puzzle. Complete the sentence by finding the missing words.

    A very brave teenager named _____ named her 1000-year-old tree _____.

2. Answer these questions.

    (a) What are a lot of trees cut down and used to make?

    (b) (i) Why was Julia outraged?

    (ii) What did she do?

    (c) List nine things people are now recycling.

    (d) What do you think the author meant by the phrase 'stop the rot'?

Prim-Ed Publishing   www.prim-ed.com   The environment   29

Teachers notes
A tree named Luna

Answers

1. Answers will vary
2. (a) 10 years old
   (b) Teacher check
   (c) 2004 and 1999
   (d) Drought
   (e) The tree may have been leaning over, perhaps due to being in a windy location or on the side of a hill.

Additional activities

- Provide an actual cross-section of a tree for the pupils to investigate and determine the history of its growing location. (DO NOT cut down a tree for this exercise.)
- Brainstorm a web of living things to describe the possible ecosystem of the 10-year-old tree in Activity 2.

Lesson outline

- Revisit the story about Julia and the reasons why she lived in her tree 'Luna' for so long. Encourage the pupils to give their opinions on whether Julia's actions were worthwhile or appropriate. Have the pupils imagine what it might have been like for her living in the tree by herself for such a long period.

- Read together the introduction at the top of the pupil activity page. Briefly brainstorm a few reasons why old-growth forests are important to their ecosystem to direct the pupils as to the types of things which might be appropriate to complete Question 1.

- Allow the pupils time to complete Question 1 independently. Once complete, the pupils can share their lists for comparison and add to their own if appropriate.

- Direct the pupils to the passage describing the ways we can use a tree to determine the history of an area. Read the passage together.

- If possible, provide an example of a tree cross-section or a large picture of one for the pupils to attempt to analyse. Make special note of different colours in the timber, wider and narrower rings and any outstanding variations in the shape of the cross-section.

- Look at the tree trunk cross-section in Question 2. Briefly discuss any outstanding features of the cross-section based on what they have just read and seen.

- Have the pupils work independently to complete parts (a) to (e) of Question 2.

- As a whole class, go through each part of Question 2 to analyse the tree trunk cross-section together.

Objectives

- Understands the part played by an old-growth forest tree in its ecosystem.
- Identifies information the rings of a tree stump can tell about climatic history.

Curriculum links

Country	Subject	Level	Objectives
England	Science	KS 2	• Know about the different plants and animals found in different habitats.
Northern Ireland	Science and technology	KS 2	• Know about the relationship between animals and plants in a habitat.
Republic of Ireland	Science	5th/6th Class	• Identify the interrelationships between plants and animals in habitats.
Scotland	Science	Level D	• Give examples of how plants and animals are suited to their environment.
Wales	Science	KS 2	• Find out about the variety of plants and animals found in different habitats.

A tree named Luna

Ancient trees – not just for me

'Luna' is a 1000-year-old tree. Imagine how many people have lived and died during Luna's lifetime! Unfortunately, trees like Luna are being cut down every day from old-growth forests. Quite often, these amazing trees are simply chipped for us to put on our garden. Our use for them does not compare to how useful they are alive to the animals and plants in an old-growth forest ecosystem.

1. Brainstorm 10 reasons why old-growth forest trees are important to their ecosystem.

   _____
   _____
   _____
   _____
   _____
   _____
   _____
   _____
   _____
   _____

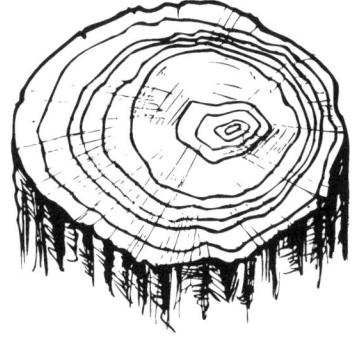

When a tree in an old-growth forest dies of natural causes such as a lightning strike or old age, it can tell us a great deal about the climatic history of the area. When we look at a tree stump we can see a series of rings. Each of these rings (made up of a lighter ring for spring growth and a darker ring for summer growth) represents the growth of a tree in one year. Luna would have 1000 of these rings! When a ring is wider, we can tell that the climatic conditions, such as higher rainfall, helped the tree grow more during that year.

2. Look at the tree stump above and answer the questions.

   (a) How old was the tree? _____

   (b) The tree fell in 2004. Write the years of growth on each ring.

   (c) What years had the heaviest rainfall? _____

   (d) What do you think may have happened during 2002? _____

   (e) The rings are wider on one side of the stump than the other. Explain why you think this may have happened.

   _____
   _____

Teachers notes
A tree named Luna

Lesson outline

- Draw the pupils' attention to the recycling programmes operating in the school and in the local community. Discuss the ways many people recycle and reuse things at home. Encourage the pupils to share ways they are recycling at home.

- Read together the information at the top of the pupil activity page. Allow the pupils to verbally answer the questions posed in the text.

- Give the pupils time to draw a diagram of their own bedroom at home. Encourage the pupils to include as much detail as possible. It may be necessary for them to draw their diagram on a separate sheet of paper. To make the activity as easily understood as possible, ensure the pupils do not colour their diagrams and use only lead pencil.

- Discuss briefly the types of things which can be recycled or reused. Allow the pupils time to colour the items which fit into these categories to complete parts (b) and (c). (Recycled—treated so a new product can be made; reused—used again in the same state.)

- Read Question 2 together and allow the pupils to complete it independently. Encourage them to share any items in their bedroom which cannot fit into any category listed. What kinds of things are they? Question the pupils. Should these things have been created in the first place? Could we live without them? Can you think of any alternative use for these items to avoid having them end up as land fill?

- Allow the pupils time to think about what to do with their 'problem' items and to write their suggestions in Question 3.

- Discuss what changes the pupils could make to their pattern of consuming in the future. Allow the pupils to complete Question 4.

Answers

1. Teacher check
2. Teacher check
3. Answers will vary
4. Answers will vary

Additional activities

- Where does waste go in your community? Use the Internet or phone books to find out.
- Where are the local recycling plants in your community?

Objective
- Identifies items in a familiar environment that can be recycled or reused.

Curriculum links

Country	Subject	Level	Objectives
England	Geography	KS 2	Recognise how people can improve the environment.
Northern Ireland	Science and technology	KS 2	Know how waste can be reduced by recycling and how this can be beneficial to the environment.
Republic of Ireland	Geography	5th/6th Class	Investigate aspects of human activities which have a positive effect on the environment; e.g. recycling and reuse of materials.
Scotland	Society	Level C	Describe ways that resources in Scotland are conserved and recycled.
Wales	Geography	KS 2	Understand the individual's responsibility for the environment; e.g. recycling.

A tree named Luna

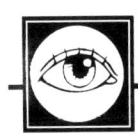

Stopping the rot

Today, many people are environmentally conscious. We recycle and reuse more than ever before. However, we are still creating waste at an alarming rate. Where is all this rubbish going? A lot of it does not break down. We cannot burn it because it pollutes the air. So it is simply buried and left forever. What a mess! How much mess do you make?

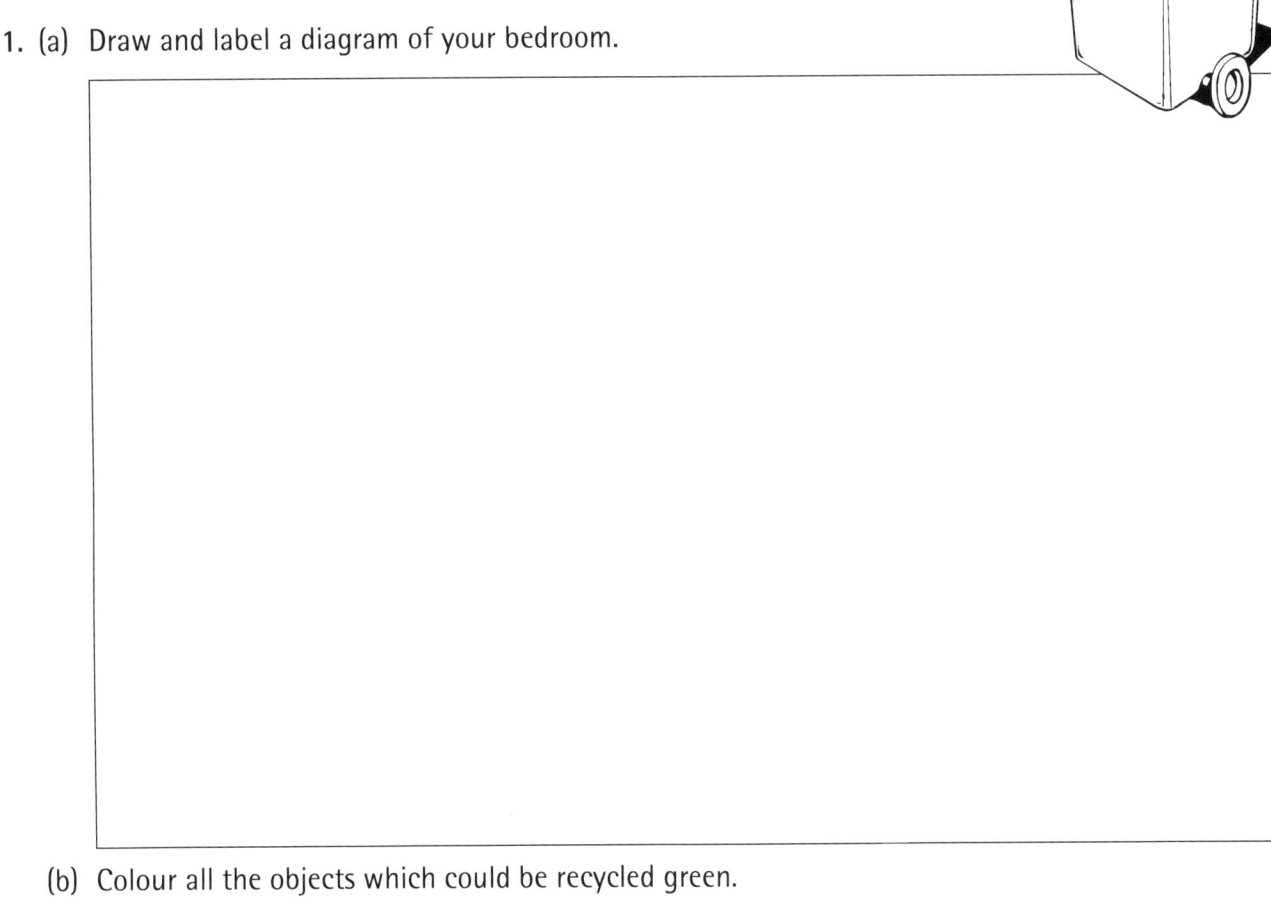

1. (a) Draw and label a diagram of your bedroom.

   (b) Colour all the objects which could be recycled green.

   (c) Colour all the objects which could be reused blue.

2. (a) Put a cross through all the objects which you will no longer have in 10 years.

   (b) Make a plan for these objects so that they will not become landfill.

   (i) If it will be recycled (parts used to make something else), write 're' next to it.

   (ii) If it will be reused by your family, write 'f' next to it.

   (iii) If it will be donated to charity to be used by someone else, write 'd' next to it.

3. (a) Do you have anything which cannot be recycled or reused? **Yes** | **No**

   (b) Can you think of any way of stopping it from becoming waste? Write your ideas.

   _____

   _____

4. What can you do to make sure you do not create waste in the future? _____

   _____

Teachers notes
Life in a greenhouse

Background information

It was over 100 years ago, in 1896, that a Swedish chemist name Svante Arrhenius first used the phrase 'the greenhouse effect'. He was concerned that as a result of the industrial revolution and the burning of fossil fuels that the amount of carbon dioxide in the atmosphere was increasing, in turn increasing climatic temperature.

Natural levels of carbon dioxide and other gases are required in the atmosphere to trap some radiated heat and prevent it from returning back into space. Earth would be 30 °C cooler without this phenomenon. Before the industrial revolution 200 years ago, carbon dioxide was about 280 parts per million (ppm). Svante Arrhenius noted 300 ppm in 1896 and now it is at least 350 ppm and increasing.

Eighty per cent of the increase in atmospheric gases is attributed to the burning of fossil fuels—i.e. the pollutant by-product. Some estimate that by 2030 the concentration of carbon dioxide will be as high as 560 ppm. By shifting to renewable energy as soon as possible, this figure may be avoided.

For island and beach communities, this change would turn out to be very significant. If global temperature increases, some polar icecaps will melt and the sea level will rise. A 1-metre rise in sea level will result in 200 million people becoming homeless. A 2-metre rise will see the Maldive Islands disappear almost completely.

Furthermore, the ecological effect of temperature rise is enormous. Plant and animal species and entire ecosystems (such as coastal communities, arctic tundra) would not be able to cope with the rapid change and would simply disappear.

Discussion points

- Why do you think a change in climatic conditions (e.g. some areas having more rain while others experience drought), could cause the extinction of many life forms?
- The author suggests that the solution to global warming is simple—just stop creating so much air pollution. Do you think this is a simple thing to achieve? Why?

Websites

http://www.epa.gov/globalwarming/kids/greenhouse.html

http://www.ucar.edu/learn/1_3_1.htm

Objective

- Reads and understands informational text about the causes of global warming and its consequences.

Curriculum links

Country	Subject	Level	Objectives
England	Literacy	Year 5	• Use evidence from a text to explain events or ideas.
		Year 6	• Understand underlying themes, causes and points of view.
Northern Ireland	Language and literacy	KS 2	• Engage in a range of reading activities.
Republic of Ireland	English	5th/6th Class	• Explore non-fiction texts and use comprehension skills.
Scotland	English	Level D	• Complete practical reading tasks.
Wales	English	KS 2	• Read for information.

Life in a greenhouse

Have you ever been to the botanical gardens and walked through a greenhouse? When you open the doors and enter, you are immediately aware that the air around you is quite warm and muggy. All the plants living in this environment are from the moist tropical areas of the world and like the hot and wet conditions. After a while it becomes a little uncomfortable in the greenhouse and when you open the door to exit, the outside air feels cool and welcoming.

These days we hear a lot about 'the greenhouse effect' on the atmosphere of the world. It is thought that the greenhouse effect may be causing global warming. But how exactly is this happening?

The atmosphere is the thin layer of air surrounding the planet. This air contains natural levels of gases, about 99% of which are held within 29 km of the Earth's surface. These gases act like a huge blanket to trap heat and keep the Earth warm—just like a greenhouse does.

So what is causing the atmosphere to heat up more than is natural? What could cause global warming? Unfortunately, it is pollution caused by human activities, increasing the amount of greenhouse gases in the atmosphere which in turn trap more heat. For example:

Human activity:	Greenhouse gas pollution created:
Burning fossil fuels; e.g. coal	carbon dioxide
Decomposing garage landfills	methane
Forest burn-offs	carbon dioxide
Refrigeration	CFCs (Chlorofluorocarbons)
Air-conditioning	CFCs (Chlorofluorocarbons)
Aerosols; e.g. hairspray cans	CFCs (Chlorofluorocarbons)
Disturbing soil for agriculture	Nitrous oxide
Adding artificial fertilisers	Nitrous oxide

(Note: The Montreal Protocol of 1991 banned the further use of CFCs.)

Because global warming would cause the polar icecaps to melt, the oceans of the world would rise. Also some areas would have more droughts and other areas would have more rain. Altogether the world would change dramatically and we would see the extinction of an enormous amount of life.

But here is a solution—we can stop creating as much air pollution by:

- using renewable energy instead of burning fossil fuels such as coal and petrol in cars,
- reducing the amount of trees being destroyed,
- halting the increase in human population.

What solutions can you come up with?

Teachers notes
Life in a greenhouse

Answers

1. (a) and (c)

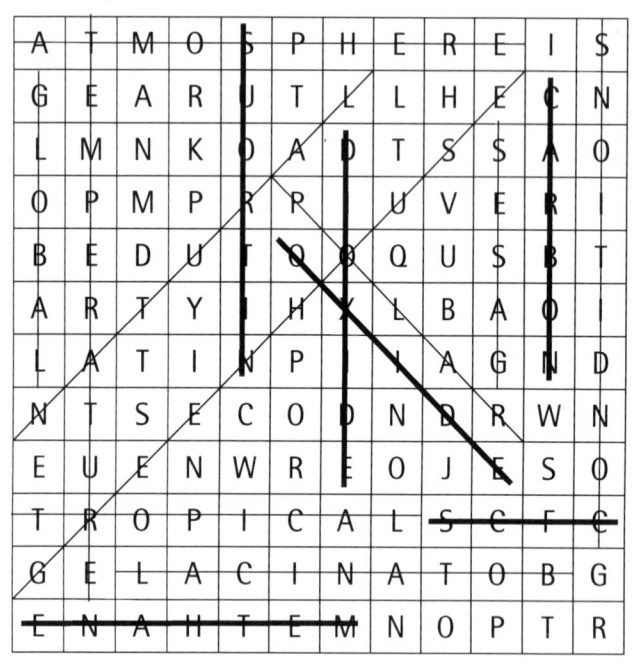

A	T	M	O	S	P	H	E	R	E	I	S
G	E	A	R	U	T	L	L	H	E	C	N
L	M	N	K	O	A	D	T	S	S	A	O
O	P	M	P	R	R	P	U	V	E	R	R
B	E	D	U	T	O	O	Q	U	S	B	T
A	R	T	Y	J	H	Y	L	B	A	O	R
L	A	T	I	N	P	L	A	G	N	D	D
N	T	S	E	C	O	O	N	R	W	N	
E	U	E	N	W	R	E	O	J	E	S	O
T	R	O	P	I	C	A	L	S	C	F	C
G	E	L	A	C	I	N	A	T	O	B	G
E	N	A	H	T	E	M	N	O	P	T	R

   (b) (i)   botany—science of structure, physiology, classification, and distribution of plants
       (ii) tropical—peculiar to, suggestive of the tropics
       (iii) polar—of or near either pole of the Earth
   (c) (i)   carbon dioxide   (ii) methane
       (iii) CFCs   (iv) nitrous oxide

2. (a) warm, humid or 'muggy'
   (b) global warming
   (c) (i)   Answers will vary
       (ii) Possibly 10 °C higher than current temperature
   (d) Answers will vary.

Objectives

- Identifies and understands the meaning of new words.
- Extracts relevant information about the greenhouse effect and global warming.

Curriculum links

Country	Subject	Level	Objectives
England	Literacy	Year 5	• Spell words and group words according to their meanings.
		Year 6	• Spell familiar words correctly and employ strategies to spell difficult words.
Northern Ireland	Language and literacy	KS 2	• Acquire and develop a vocabulary.
Republic of Ireland	English	5th/6th Class	• Extend and develop vocabulary and spelling.
Scotland	English	Level D/E	• Know specialist vocabulary from different curricular areas.
Wales	English	KS 2	• Use their knowledge gained from reading to develop their vocabulary.

Life in a greenhouse

1. **Complete these activities.**

   (a) Find each new word in the puzzle.

   New words
   - botanical
   - tropical
   - atmosphere
   - natural
   - temperature
   - greenhouse
   - conditions
   - global
   - gases
   - polar

A	T	M	O	S	P	H	E	R	E	I	S
G	E	A	R	U	T	L	L	H	E	C	N
L	M	N	K	O	A	D	T	S	S	A	O
O	P	M	P	R	P	I	U	V	E	R	I
B	E	D	U	T	O	O	Q	U	S	B	T
A	R	T	Y	I	H	X	L	B	A	O	I
L	A	T	I	N	P	I	I	A	G	N	D
N	T	S	E	C	O	D	N	D	R	W	N
E	U	E	N	W	R	E	O	J	E	S	O
T	R	O	P	I	C	A	L	S	C	F	C
G	E	L	A	C	I	N	A	T	O	B	G
E	N	A	H	T	E	M	N	O	P	T	R

   (b) Write meanings for these words. Use a dictionary to help you.

   (i) botany _____

   (ii) tropical _____

   (iii) polar _____

   (c) There are four different types of greenhouse gas pollution hidden in the puzzle above. Can you find them?

   (i) c_____ d_____
   (ii) m_____
   (iii) _____ (chlorofluorocarbons)
   (iv) n_____ o_____

2. **Answer these questions.**

   (a) What is the atmosphere like in a greenhouse? _____

   (b) What is the 'greenhouse effect' said to be causing? _____

   (c) (i) What is the temperature in your classroom today? _____

   (ii) What do you think the temperature in your classroom would be if there were no greenhouse gases? _____

   (d) Describe why you think global warming would be so devastating. _____

Teachers notes
Life in a greenhouse

Answers

1. Teacher check
2. (a) Warmer
   (b) The icecubes will melt.
   (c) The melted icecubes submerged the 'land' in the greenhouse.
3. Answers will vary

Additional activities

- Create a class terrarium of tropical plants to live in greenhouse conditions similar to the climatic conditions that might be found on the Equator.
- On a world map, shade the areas of the world which may become uninhabitable if the temperature of the world were 10 °C higher. Consider also loss of land due to an increase in sea level.

Lesson outline

- Review what a greenhouse is. Discuss the practical uses of greenhouses for propagation of plants and the growing of particular species. Have the pupils suggest ways in which greenhouses could be useful.

- Encourage the pupils to share their experiences of being inside a greenhouse. Have them describe how it felt, smelt and looked. Discuss what it might be like to live in a greenhouse all the time or to live in the tropics or near the Equator.

- Use a globe to show where the Equator is and the zones between it and the tropics. Identify some of the countries in that area and have the pupils recall and share what they know about these countries.

- Explain to the pupils that they will be simulating the conditions in a greenhouse by making a miniature version. Direct them to the instructions on the pupil activity page and read them together carefully as a group so the pupils know not only how to build their greenhouse, but what the purpose of the activity is (to demonstrate that air trapped within a greenhouse gradually becomes hotter and hotter in the sun).

- Ensure there are ample resources prior to the lesson for the pupils to build their greenhouses.

- Allow the pupils time to construct their greenhouses and make their initial observation.

- Have the pupils make quick observations after 30 minutes and after 1 hour. Discuss these general observations.

- Direct the pupils to Question 2. Allow them to answer 2(a) based on their observations and to then place icecubes in their greenhouses to complete 2(b).

- Allow the pupils to sit and observe what happens to the 'land' in the model as the icecubes melt. Have the pupils write their answers to 2(c) to explain their observations.

- Discuss what might happen if the whole globe was subjected to the greenhouse effect in such a way. What would happen to the polar icecaps? What would happen to existing land masses? Would a rise in water level affect them and where they live? How would an increase in temperature affect them? Do they think they would have an increase or a decrease in rainfall where they live? Why?

- Allow the pupils to complete Question 3 independently. Give the pupils an opportunity to share their ideas with their peers.

Objective

- Investigates how a greenhouse works by making a model.

Curriculum links

Country	Subject	Level	Objectives
England	Science	KS 2	Make observations and communicate data in an appropriate manner.
Northern Ireland	Science and technology	KS 2	Record, analyse and present in appropriate ways.
Republic of Ireland	Science	5th/6th Class	Carry out simple experiments and record and present findings.
Scotland	Science	Level C	Make a short report of an investigation.
Wales	Science	KS 2	Make careful observations and record them appropriately.

Life in a greenhouse

The greenhouse experiment

1. Investigate how a greenhouse works by making your own.

   (a) Find the following materials:
   - A flat stone—to represent land
   - A glass jar—to represent the atmosphere (the glass represents the blanket of greenhouse gases trapping heat from the sun)
   - Fresh leaves—to represent plant life
   - Water—to represent the ocean

   (b) Put your greenhouse together as shown in the diagram.

   (c) Find a place in full sun to put your 'greenhouse'.

   (d) Write your observations:

After 5 minutes	
After 30 minutes	
After one hour	

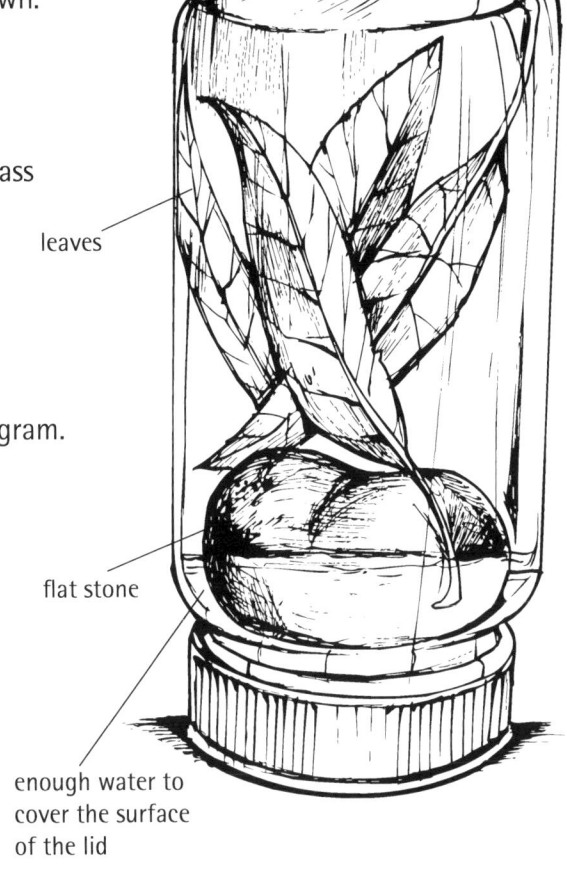

   Diagram labels: glass jar turned upside down; leaves; flat stone; enough water to cover the surface of the lid

2. (a) Open your greenhouse and feel the temperature inside. Is it warmer or cooler than the air outside the bottle?

   Warmer | **Cooler**

   (b) Place icecubes in your greenhouse to represent the polar icecaps. What do you think will happen to them in the warm greenhouse?

   _____

   _____

   (c) How has the melting of the icecubes affected the land in the greenhouse?

   _____

   _____

3. Think about where you live. If the world's temperature was 10 °C warmer all year round, predict how your local environment would change.

Prim-Ed Publishing   www.prim-ed.com   **The environment**   39

Teachers notes
Life in a greenhouse

Lesson outline

- Ask the pupils whether they consider themselves to be contributing to air pollution in their daily lives. If so, have them give examples of the air pollution they are producing and how they are producing it.

- Have the pupils discuss who they think are the main contributors to air pollution.

- Read together the information at the top of the pupil activity page. Revise our basic needs to survive. Ask the pupils to reconsider their contribution to air pollution. Do they think there are things they could be doing to reduce the amount of air pollution they are creating?

- Introduce the survey in Question 1 to the pupils. Read through the 'pollution-creating things' list and the scale describing whether or not they are things the pupils could live without.

- Briefly demonstrate an appropriate way to tally the data they collect. Have the pupils practise by completing the survey themselves before interviewing their classmates. Allow the pupils time to conduct their survey.

- Discuss the general results of their survey. Have the pupils suggest how their data could be better arranged (in graphs etc.) to explain the results.

- Have the pupils read Question 2, analyse their data and complete parts (a), (b) and (c).

- Question the pupils about what they think could be done to reduce pollution. What would have the greatest impact? What would be the greatest obstacles preventing a reduction in greenhouse gases in the future?

- Read together Question 2(d) and give the pupils time to think and write what they consider would be the most important thing they could invent to reduce greenhouse gases.

- Give the pupils an opportunity to share their innovative ideas.

Answers

1. Teacher check
2. (a) Teacher check
   (b) Teacher check
   (c) Answers will vary
   (d) Teacher check

Additional activities

- Use the data from the survey on the pupil activity sheet to plot three bar graphs. Title the graphs 'Couldn't live without it', 'Could reduce how much I use it', and 'Could live without it'.

- Have the pupils describe a lifestyle using the minimum amount of pollution-creating items they would be prepared to live with. Encourage them to evaluate, on a scale of 1 to 10, how their lifestyle would impact upon the environment.

Objective

- Conducts a survey to investigate whether peers can or cannot live without or reduce the use of pollution-creating 'wants'.

Curriculum links

Country	Subject	Level	Objectives
England	Geography	KS 2	• Recognise how and why people may seek to manage environments sustainably and to identify opportunities for their own involvement.
Northern Ireland	Geography	KS 2	• Know about some of the ways people affect/conserve the environment.
Republic of Ireland	Geography/Science	5th/6th Class	• Come to appreciate individual responsibility for environmental care.
Scotland	Science	Level D	• Describe examples of human impact on the environment that have brought about beneficial changes and detrimental effects.
Wales	Geography	KS 2	• Understand the individual's responsibility for the environment.

Life in a greenhouse

Simple solutions

We are creating far too much air pollution, by burning fossil fuels like coal to make energy, burning off rubbish and forests, using refrigeration, airconditioners and aerosol cans and by using fertilisers. In our society, most of us believe we 'need' to do or use all of these things. However, most of these are 'wants'. What we really 'need' is clean air to breathe and a decrease in greenhouse gases!

1. Conduct a survey to find out whether the pupils in your class would be willing to live without, or reduce their use of, the following pollution creating items. Don't forget to complete the survey yourself!

Pollution-creating item	I couldn't live without it	I could reduce how much I use it	I could live without it
(a) television			
(b) airconditioner			
(c) refrigerator			
(d) spray-on deodorant			
(e) computer			
(f) fireplace			
(g) hairspray			
(h) electricity			
(i) car			
(j) hot water			
(k) plastic bags			

2. Analysing the data

   (a) What things do most pupils think they could not live without?

   (b) What things would the pupils be most likely to live without?

   (c) Based on these results, do you think it is likely that greenhouse gases will be greatly reduced by your generation?

   Yes   No

   (d) If you were an inventor, what do you think would be the most important thing you could invent to help reduce greenhouse gases?

   _____

   _____

   _____

Teachers notes
Biodiversity

Background information

Biodiversity is defined as 'the variety of life forms: the different plants, animals and micro-organisms, the genes they contain, and the ecosystems they form. It is usually considered at three levels; genetic diversity, species diversity and ecosystem diversity'. Retaining biodiversity is vital from both an instrumental and intrinsic or ethical perspective. The fact that we are losing plant and animal species to extinction at an alarmingly rapid pace is genuine cause for concern and immediate action.

Part of the concern lies in how little we know about most of the world's natural wealth. Only about 1.75 million plant and animal species have been formally identified, and very few of those have ever been studied in detail. As each life form on Earth has its own set of unique features, the value and importance each plays to life on Earth, and indeed to humans, is neverending. But herein lies the problem. As the extinction rates and loss of biodiversity increase, the potential of life on Earth decreases.

As each life form is scientifically identified, it is given a formal classification under the rules of taxonomy. So each plant and animal species has a scientific name derived from the ancient language of Latin. Greek derivatives are also used. By using an ancient or 'dead' language, interpreters are assured that definitions do not change over time. Because scientific names are quite difficult for laypeople to remember, many species are also given common names.

Back in the 1700s, Carl von Linne, a Swedish botanist, developed a system of nomenclature (systematic naming) using Latin and Greek roots. It is a binominal system; i.e. every plant and animal species must have two names. This system is known as Linnean classification, with the first name being generic (the genus—a group of closely-related plants or animals) and the second being the specific name of the actual species.

Using the Linnean classification system of nomenclature, the koala has been scientifically named Phascolarctos cinereus. Koala is the common name. The genus is Phascolarctos and the species is cinereus. Note that scientific names are italicised or underlined and all species names start in lower case. The meaning is derived from phaskolos, Greek for 'pouch', arktos, Greek for 'bear', and cineris, Latin for 'ashes' or 'ash-coloured'. Therefore, when the koala was scientifically named by Goldfuss in 1817, he thought words to the effect of 'pouched-bear ashy-coloured' were a good definition. Today we know that koalas are not related to bears; however, the scientific name tries to reflect the characteristics of the species.

Discussion points

- Why do we need such a wide variety of different species?
- Does it matter if we lose a few animals, insects and plants?
- Why do you think some people are apathetic about ensuring biodiversity?

Websites

http://www.nd.edu/~archives/latgramm.htm
(Latin)

http://www.nbn.org.uk/
(National Biodiversity Betwork)

http://www.naturegrid.org.uk/biodiversity/galindex.html

Objective
- Reads and understands informational text about the loss of biodiversity.

Curriculum links

Country	Subject	Level	Objectives
England	Literacy	Year 5	• Use evidence from a text to explain events or ideas.
		Year 6	• Understand underlying themes, causes and points of view.
Northern Ireland	Language and literacy	KS 2	• Engage in a range of reading activities.
Republic of Ireland	English	5th/6th Class	• Explore non-fiction texts and use comprehension skills.
Scotland	English	Level D	• Complete practical reading tasks.
Wales	English	KS 2	• Read for information.

Biodiversity

Lots of scientific and medical words are derived from the ancient language 'Latin'. By using Latin we know that the terms will always mean the same. Our language is living, it changes little by little; for example, we know that 'bangers and mash' means sausages and potatoes. The nicknames have now become an understood part of our language. But Latin does not change.

For example, 'bio' in Latin means life. So the word biodiversity means 'life diversity'. And we have a remarkable amount of life diversity on earth. Humans are one species of a group of approximately 4300 mammal species on earth. (The scientific Latin name for the human species is homo sapiens meaning homo—man, sapere—to be wise). There are approximately 9000 species of birds, 4250 species of amphibians and 7000 species of reptiles. However, more than 95% of animal species are invertebrates (they do not have a backbone), like insects and spiders, molluscs and sponges. If you add to that all the plant species we have in the world, estimates have been made that there are probably between 13 and 14 million different life forms, but there could be as many as 100 million.

All species are fascinating and important in their own way, all with their own unique way of life and each individual with its own behaviours and features as different as we are.

So what's all the fuss about the 'loss of biodiversity' that everyone keeps talking about?

- At the moment we are experiencing an extinction spasm caused by human activities.
- The extent of these extinctions has been estimated at between 1000 and 75 000 species of plants and animals per year.
- The major impact for species is through habitat loss. In Australia, over 80% of the 1430 species of animals listed as threatened are in that situation due to habitat loss.
- Between 40% and 50% of the land on earth has been disturbed and degraded already by humans.
- It is estimated that one-third of the world's natural capital was lost between 1970 and 1995.

This is pretty scary stuff. No wonder species are finding it hard to survive out there. Is it time for us to save the planet?

Teachers notes
Biodiversity

Answers

1. (a) and (c)

E	T	A	R	B	E	T	R	E	V	N	I
A	L	Y	C	S	U	L	L	O	M	B	W
T	J	A	T	F	P	S	M	I	A	P	
R	E	P	T	I	L	E	V	P	N	T	S
S	L	Q	A	I	S	T	C	N	G	U	E
P	A	K	T	U	N	R	L	I	S	Q	R
H	M	L	I	F	E	X	E	O	E	N	P
Z	M	V	B	D	O	T	R	V	N	S	T
E	A	R	A	C	W	E	U	Q	I	N	U
A	M	P	H	I	B	I	A	N	O	D	C

(b) (i) diverse—unlike in nature of qualities, varied
(ii) unique—of which there is only one
(iii) habitat—natural home of plant or animal

(c) (i) life (ii) man (iii) wise

2. (a) Latin does not change because it is not a 'living' language and does not change over time, unlike English which is currently in use and subject to change.

(b) Biodiversity means life diversity.

(c) Homo sapien means 'wise man'.

(d) The number of life forms on earth is only an estimate because many species may yet be undiscovered and the number of species becoming extinct is too high and occurring too rapidly to give an accurate count.

(e) 'Natural capital' refers to natural elements of extrinsic and intrinsic value to humans.

Objectives
- Identifies and understands the meaning of new words.
- Extracts relevant information about the loss of biodiversity.

Curriculum links

Country	Subject	Level	Objectives
England	Literacy	Year 5	• Spell words and group words according to their meanings.
		Year 6	• Spell familiar words correctly and employ strategies to spell difficult words.
Northern Ireland	Language and literacy	KS 2	• Acquire and develop a vocabulary.
Republic of Ireland	English	5th/6th Class	• Extend and develop vocabulary and spelling.
Scotland	English	Level D/E	• Know specialist vocabulary from different curricular areas.
Wales	English	KS 2	• Use their knowledge gained from reading to develop their vocabulary.

Biodiversity

1. Complete these activities.

    (a) Find each new word in the puzzle.

    New words
    - Latin
    - mammal
    - reptile
    - species
    - unique
    - diversity
    - amphibian
    - mollusc
    - invertebrate

E	T	A	R	B	E	T	R	E	V	N	I
A	L	Y	C	S	U	L	L	O	M	B	W
T	J	A	T	F	P	S	M	I	A	P	I
R	E	P	T	I	L	E	V	P	N	T	S
S	L	Q	A	I	S	T	C	N	G	U	E
P	A	K	T	U	N	R	L	I	S	Q	R
H	M	L	I	F	E	X	E	O	E	N	P
Z	M	V	B	D	O	T	R	V	N	S	T
E	A	R	A	C	W	E	U	Q	I	N	U
A	M	P	H	I	B	I	A	N	O	D	C

    (b) Write meanings for these words. Use a dictionary to help you.

      (i) diverse _____

      (ii) unique _____

      (iii) habitat _____

    (c) There are three Latin word meanings hidden in the puzzle. Can you find them? Use the Latin words below to help you.

      (i) 'bio' means _____
      (ii) 'homo' means _____
      (iii) 'sapere' means to be _____

2. Answer these questions.

    (a) Why doesn't the language Latin change over time like English?

    (b) What does 'biodiversity' mean?

    (c) What does 'homo sapien' mean?

    (d) Why is the number of life forms on earth only an estimate?

    (e) What do you think is meant by the world's 'natural capital'?

Teachers notes
Biodiversity

Answers
1. (a) ash-coloured bear with pouch
   (b) wise man
   (c) red, large-footed animal
   (d) grey-headed and wing-footed
   (e) southern land
2. (a) rufus cephalus polio ptero
   (b) Answers will vary

Additional activities
- Imagine you are a scientist interested in biology. You need to know all about biology—the study of life. In biology, there are many terms not commonly used. Find the meanings of these biodiverse terms:
  Vertebrate—*any animal that has a spine*
  Invertebrate—*any animal that does not have a spine*
  Endotherm—*animal capable of maintaining body temperature above the temperature of the external environment*
  Ectotherm—*cold-blooded animal, which cannot regulate its body temperature*
  Mollusc—*animal with soft body and usually a hard shell, such as a snail, cuttlefish and oyster*
  Arachnid—*spider, scorpion, tick, mite (from the family Arachnida)*
  Photosynthesis—*a process possible in the presence of light where CO_2 and water are converted into oxygen or organic materials that can be used in the plant*
  Arboreal—*an animal that is designed to live primarily in trees*
  Symbiosis—*association of two different organisms living attached to each other or one with the other*

Objectives
- Understands the origins of scientific names for animals and plants.
- Deciphers the meaning of a selection of scientific names.

Lesson outline
- Review what is meant by a 'living' language. Discuss why it is important that scientific language not be 'living'. Read together the introductory passage at the top of the pupil activity page.
- Introduce the pupils to the list of scientific Latin or Greek words and their meanings in Question 1. Look at 1 (a) and work out the meaning of the koala's scientific name together.
- Allow the pupils to complete parts (b) to (e) independently.
- Read the italic passage which follows together.
- Have the pupils refer to the Latin and Greek words in question 1 to complete their description in Question 2.
- Encourage the pupils to share the common (English) names for their butterfly.
- If time permits, provide textbooks for the pupils to peruse and locate the scientific names of a selection of well-known animals. Encourage the pupils to try to decipher what the words in their scientific name might be describing about each animal.

Background information
The table below is an extension of that used in the pupil activity to assist teachers in clarifying terminology.

Latin or Greek word	Modified word	Meaning
arktos (Gr)	arctos	bear
australis (L)	australis	southern
kephale (Gr)	cephalus	head
cineris (L)	cinereus	ashes, ash-coloured
homo (L)	homo	man
makros (Gr)	macro	large
phaskolos (Gr)	phascol	pouch
polio (L)	polio	grey
pous (Gr)	pus	foot
ptero (Gr)	ptero	wing
rufus (L)	rufus	red
sapere (L)	sapiens	to be wise
terra (L)	terra	land

Curriculum links

Country	Subject	Level	Objectives
England	Science	KS 2	Know animals can be identified and assigned to groups.
Northern Ireland	Science and technology	KS 2	Classify animals according to observable features.
Republic of Ireland	Science	5th/6th Class	Group living things into sets according to their similarities and differences.
Scotland	Science	Level C	Name animals using simple keys.
Wales	Science	KS 2	Know animals can be identified and assigned to groups.

Biodiversity

A scientific language

Latin is not spoken today, but is used in science and medicine throughout the world to give common-ground meanings to species names and medical terms. Another language also used for this purpose is Greek.

Latin or Greek word	Meaning
arctos	bear
australis	southern
cephalus	head
cinereus	ashes, ash-coloured
homo	man
macro	large
phascol	pouch
polio	grey
pus	foot
ptero	wing
rufus	red
sapiens	to be wise
terra	land

1. Look at the list of Latin and Greek words. See if you can work out what the scientific names mean.

Common name	Scientific name	Meaning
(a) Koala	*Phascolarctos cinereus*	_____
(b) Human	*Homo sapiens*	_____
(c) Red kangaroo	*Macropus rufus*	_____
(d) Grey-headed flying-fox	*Pteropus poliocephalus*	_____
(e) Australia	*Terra australis*	_____

Many plants and animals are yet to be described and have no common name and no scientific name. One day you may become a scientist helping protect biodiversity and you might be honoured by naming a previously unknown species.

2. (a) If you came across a new butterfly that had a red head and grey wings, what Latin words could you use in its name to describe the creature?

   _____   _____   _____   _____
   red   head   grey   wing

   (b) What would be a good common (English) name for the butterfly?

Teachers notes
Biodiversity

Lesson outline

- Discuss 'revolutions' the pupils have heard about. Read the definition of a revolution at the top of the pupil activity page and discuss what it might be like to be part of a revolution.

- Debate whether the pupils think a nature revolution is necessary and if so whether or not it would be possible. Direct the pupils to complete Question 1.

- Brainstorm reasons why we need a nature revolution. Have the pupils use examples from the class list to inspire them to write the signs in Question 2. Encourage the pupils to read out the signs they chose to write and to explain why they felt these were the most important issues to 'picket'.

- As a whole class, recall organisations which would not benefit from a nature revolution. List some of these groups in the table in Question 3. Have the pupils write the reasons for their opposition to complete the table.

- Allow the pupils to work in pairs to brainstorm a list of points which could be used to convince one of the groups listed in the table in Question 3 to change their views and support a nature revolution. The pupils can then work collaboratively to produce a speech to present to the class.

- After each pair has presented their speech, the class should be invited to pretend they are a member of the opposing organisation and to state whether or not they would change their views.

Answers

1. Answers will vary
2. Teacher check
3. Teacher check, answers will vary
4. Answers will vary

Additional activities

- Give the pupils the opportunity to present their speech compelling their peers to embark on a nature revolution.

- Debate the merits of protesting. Have the pupils suggest other, potentially more effective ways to get their message across to the community or to government groups.

Objective

- Discusses and writes reasons for and against participation in a 'nature revolution'.

Curriculum links

Country	Subject	Level	Objectives
England	Geography	KS 2	Identify and explain different views that people hold about topical geographical issues.
Northern Ireland	Geography	KS 2	Know some of the ways people affect/conserve the environment.
Republic of Ireland	Geography/Science	5th/6th Class	Identify and discuss a global environmental issue.
Scotland	Health	Level E	Identify global environmental issues.
Wales	Geography	KS 2	Recognise that different people have different views about changes made to the environment.

Biodiversity

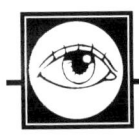

The nature revolution

'Revolution' is a word used to describe a great change or a complete turnaround.

1. Do you think we need a 'nature revolution'? **Yes** | **No**

2. What sorts of things do you think would need to change if there was a nature revolution? Use the signs to write or illustrate your ideas.

3. Can you think of any groups or organisations which would not support a nature revolution? Write them below. Complete the table by writing a reason why each would not be supportive.

Group or organisation	Reason why it may not support a nature revolution.

4. Imagine you are a politician promoting a nature revolution. Write a short speech to try to convince one of these groups to change.

Teachers notes
Threatened species

Background information

The World Conservation Union (IUCN) has status categories for listing threatened species—plants and animals—as follows:

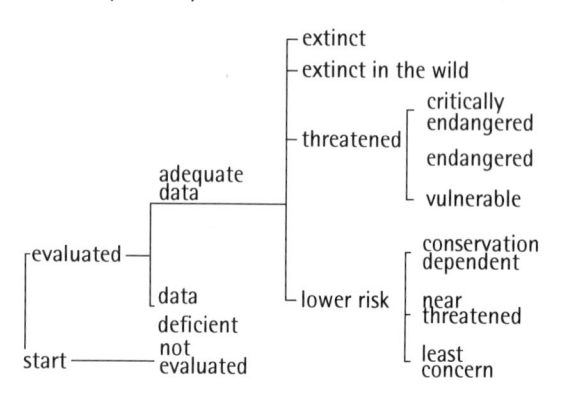

```
                                    ┌─ extinct
                                    ├─ extinct in the wild
                                    │              ┌─ critically endangered
                                    ├─ threatened ─┤── endangered
                      ┌─ adequate ──┤              └─ vulnerable
                      │    data     │              ┌─ conservation dependent
         ┌─ evaluated─┤             └─ lower risk ─┤── near threatened
         │            │                            └─ least concern
         │            └─ data deficient
start ───┤
         └─ not evaluated
```

This structure allows for greater understanding of the status and subsequent level of urgency and action required for various threatened species.

When looking at the table of threatened species, 24% or 1137 of the 4763 mammal species on earth are threatened. But these threatened mammals fall under different categories. For example, the grey-headed flying-fox (Pteropus poliocephalus) has recently been listed as 'vulnerable'. There are many thousands alive, but their numbers have declined significantly from previously due to habitat loss and human persecution. This decline is enough cause for concern that they be listed as a threatened species, thereby giving their habitats greater protection.

On the more extreme end of threatened species is the northern hairy-nosed wombat (Lasiorhinus krefftii). With only just over 100 individuals remaining in this species, the situation is quite obviously dire and they are appropriately listed as 'critically endangered'.

There are many ways that plants and animals are threatened. Some are threatened by only one negative influence, but usually it is a combination of factors. It is vitally important that we ascertain what the causes are so that solutions can be found quickly, and thus will ensure that biodiversity can be retained.

Discussion points

- What are the reasons behind labelling certain species as endangered or threatened?
- What is the likelihood of the threatened species list reducing in number? Why do you think this?

Websites

http://www.iucnredlist.org/

http://www.environment.gov.au/biodiversity/threatened/

Objectives

- Reads and understands informational text about why animal and plant species are threatened.
- Reads and understands informational text about ways species are being helped to increase in number.

Curriculum links

Country	Subject	Level	Objectives
England	Literacy	Year 5	• Use evidence from a text to explain events or ideas.
		Year 6	• Understand underlying themes, causes and points of view.
Northern Ireland	Language and literacy	KS 2	• Engage in a range of reading activities.
Republic of Ireland	English	5th/6th Class	• Explore non-fiction texts and use comprehension skills.
Scotland	English	Level D	• Complete practical reading tasks.
Wales	English	KS 2	• Read for information.

Threatened species

If an animal species or plant species is threatened, it means that the number of this species has declined so much that we are worried about its long-term survival. Once a species is listed as endangered, its chances are even further reduced. At this point there are not many individuals left and most of their habitat has been destroyed.

The following table shows the number of threatened species on the world conservation union (IUCN) 'red list' for 2002.

	Total number of species	% under threat	Actual number of species threatened
Mammals	4763	24%	1137
Birds	9946	12%	1192
Amphibians	4950	3%	157
Reptiles	7970	4%	293

Furthermore, countless fish, insects, molluscs, crustaceans and plants are also under threat.

Here are some of the ways species are threatened:

- Habitat loss
- Competition with introduced species that should not be there
- Poaching for illegal trade in animal parts
- Pollution

So what is being done to help all these threatened species? What can we do?

Here are some of the ways species are being helped:

- Scientists are studying the habitat and living needs of animals and plants so we can better understand how to help them.
- National laws are being made to stop people within a country doing the wrong thing.
- International treaties (laws between countries) are being made to stop things like the illegal trade in animal parts.
- Restoring degraded habitats.
- Lowering air and water pollution.
- Captive breeding programmes in zoos.

Teachers notes
Threatened species

Answers

1. (a) and (c)

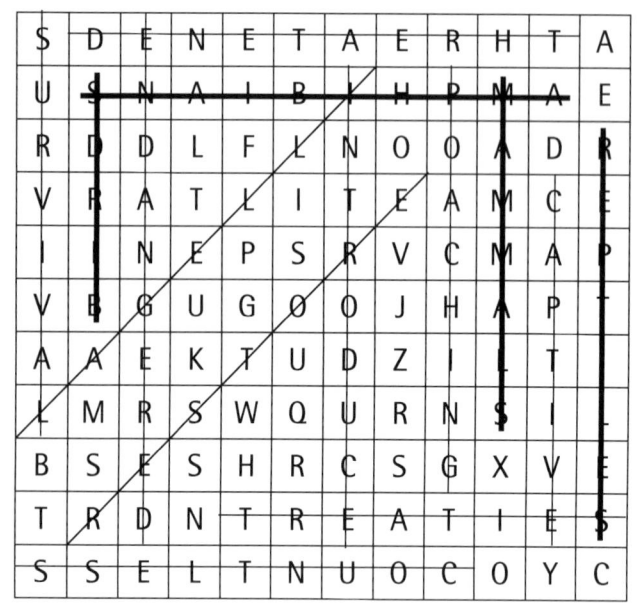

S	D	E	N	E	T	A	E	R	H	T	A
U	S	N	A	I	B	I	H	P	M	A	E
R	D	D	L	F	L	N	O	O	A	D	R
V	R	A	T	L	I	T	E	A	M	C	E
I	I	N	E	P	S	R	V	C	M	A	P
V	B	G	U	G	O	O	J	H	A	P	
A	A	E	K	T	U	D	Z	I	L	T	
L	M	R	S	W	Q	U	R	N	S	I	
B	S	E	S	H	R	C	S	G	X	V	E
T	R	D	N	T	R	E	A	T	I	E	S
S	S	E	L	T	N	U	O	C	O	Y	C

   (b) (i) introduce—bring in, place in, insert
       (ii) treaties—formally concluded and ratified agreements between independent parties etc.
       (iii) captive—taken prisoner, kept in confinement, under restraint, unable to escape
   (c) (i) mammals
       (ii) birds
       (iii) amphibians
       (iv) reptiles

2. (a) When a species is threatened it means that the number of this species has declined so much that we are worried about its long-term survival.
   (b) Habitat loss; competition with introduced species that should not be there; poaching for illegal trade in animal parts; pollution
   (c) More than 10 000
   (d) (i) Scientists help threatened species by studying the habitat and living needs of animals and plants so that we can better understand how to help them.
       (ii) Politicians help threatened species by making national laws to stop people within a country mistreating them and by creating international treaties to stop things like the illegal trade in animal parts.

Objectives

- Identifies and understands the meaning of new words.
- Extracts relevant information about threatened species.

Curriculum links

Country	Subject	Level	Objectives
England	Literacy	Year 5	• Spell words and group words according to their meanings.
		Year 6	• Spell familiar words correctly and employ strategies to spell difficult words.
Northern Ireland	Language and literacy	KS 2	• Acquire and develop a vocabulary.
Republic of Ireland	English	5th/6th Class	• Extend and develop vocabulary and spelling.
Scotland	English	Level D/E	• Know specialist vocabulary from different curricular areas.
Wales	English	KS 2	• Use their knowledge gained from reading to develop their vocabulary.

Threatened species

1. **Complete these activities.**

   (a) Find each new word in the puzzle.

   New words
   - threatened
   - endangered
   - introduce
   - illegal
   - restore
   - survival
   - countless
   - poaching
   - treaties
   - captive

S	D	E	N	E	T	A	E	R	H	T	A
U	S	N	A	I	B	I	H	P	M	A	E
R	D	D	L	F	L	N	O	O	A	D	R
V	R	A	T	L	I	T	E	A	M	C	E
I	I	N	E	P	S	R	V	C	M	A	P
V	B	G	U	G	O	O	J	H	A	P	T
A	A	E	K	T	U	D	Z	I	L	T	I
L	M	R	S	W	Q	U	R	N	S	I	L
B	S	E	S	H	R	C	S	G	X	V	E
T	R	D	N	T	R	E	A	T	I	E	S
S	S	E	L	T	N	U	O	C	O	Y	C

   (b) Write meanings for these words. Use a dictionary to help you.

   (i) introduce _____

   (ii) treaties _____

   (iii) captive _____

   (c) There are four types of animal hidden in the puzzle which match the percentages of each that are under threat. Can you find them?

   (i) 24% of m _____
   (ii) 12% of b _____
   (iii) 3% of a _____
   (iv) 4% of r _____

2. **Answer these questions.**

   (a) What does it mean when a species is 'threatened'?
   _____
   _____

   (b) List four ways a species may be threatened.
   (i) _____
   (ii) _____
   (iii) _____
   (iv) _____

   (c) Estimate how many species in the world are threatened and circle the closest answer.

   4000   5000   10 000   more than 10 000

   (d) How could these people help threatened species?

   (i) scientists _____
   _____
   _____

   (ii) politicians _____
   _____
   _____

Prim-Ed Publishing   www.prim-ed.com   The environment   53

Teachers notes
Threatened species

Answers

1. temperature— >30 °C
   rainfall—high
   ground cover—ferny undergrowth
   vegetation—large established trees with buttress roots, ferns, palms, broad-leafed plants
   topography—mountainous
   waterways—many shallow streams and waterfalls
   sunlight—filtered

2. (a) canopy; Answers will vary
   (b) leaf litter or mulch; Answers will vary
   (c) understorey; Answers will vary
   (d) stream; Answers will vary

3. Teacher check

Additional activities

- Create a diorama of a typical rainforest or another unique environment, labelling the many habitats within it.
- Research a threatened species to find out how it came to be threatened.

Objectives

- Describes the features of a rainforest.
- Recognises living things found in various rainforest habitats.
- Discuss how particular threats might affect rainforest habitats.

Lesson outline

- Review what is meant by a habitat. Have the pupils brainstorm a list of habitats and draw an explosion chart where they can see the ecosystem in which each habitat might be found. For example, a sandy habitat might be found in a desert or in coastal dunes. This will also serve the purpose of demonstrating the difference between an ecosystem and a habitat.
- Read together the introduction at the top of the pupil activity page. Explain that a rainforest is an ecosystem and that many habitats are found within it.
- Have pupils close their eyes and imagine they are walking through a rainforest. What can they see? Hear? Smell? Encourage them to describe the air, temperature and general atmosphere of the rainforest they are imagining.
- When the pupils open their eyes again, have them record their description of a rainforest under the headings given in the table for Question 1.
- Provide a stimulus picture of a rainforest which shows each of the layers within it, including ground cover, low plants, larger trees, canopy and so on. Encourage the pupils to identify different habitats in each of the layers of the rainforest.
- Direct the pupils to the pictures in Question 2. Have them identify the habitat each drawing is describing and list living things they think might be found there.
- Allow the pupils to share their interpretation of the diagrams and the associated animals and plants with the class.
- Break the class into groups of 4 or 5. Allocate each group one of the discussion topics in Question 3 (habitat loss, competition with introduced species, poaching, pollution). Have the pupils highlight the topic they are to discuss on their own activity sheet.
- Explain to the groups that they are to discuss how the threat they have been given would affect a rainforest and the habitats within it. Have each group nominate a recorder to write notes from the group discussion ready to be presented to the class.
- Have each group choose a spokesperson to present their ideas to the class for discussion.

Curriculum links

Country	Subject	Level	Objectives
England	Science	KS 2	• Know about the different plants and animals found in different habitats.
Northern Ireland	Science and technology	KS 2	• Know about the relationship between animals and plants in a habitat.
Republic of Ireland	Science	5th/6th Class	• Recognise that there is a great diversity of plants and animals in different regions and environments.
Scotland	Science	Level D	• Give examples of how animals and plants are suited to their environment.
Wales	Science	KS 2	• Find out about the variety of plants and animals found in different habitats.

Threatened species

Habitats in a rainforest – close up

A habitat is all the elements combined to make a suitable home for a creature to live. Some habitats are home to thousands of living things. A rainforest contains habitats which are special in this way.

1. Imagine you are walking through a rainforest. Use the table as a guide for describing the unique features of this environment.

temperature	
rainfall	
ground cover	
vegetation	
topography (shape of the land)	
waterways	
light	

This environment is made up of many habitats. For example, old fallen trees provide the perfect habitat for burrowing animals, fungi and moss.

2. What other habitats can you think of? List some of the living things you might find in each (use the pictures below as clues).

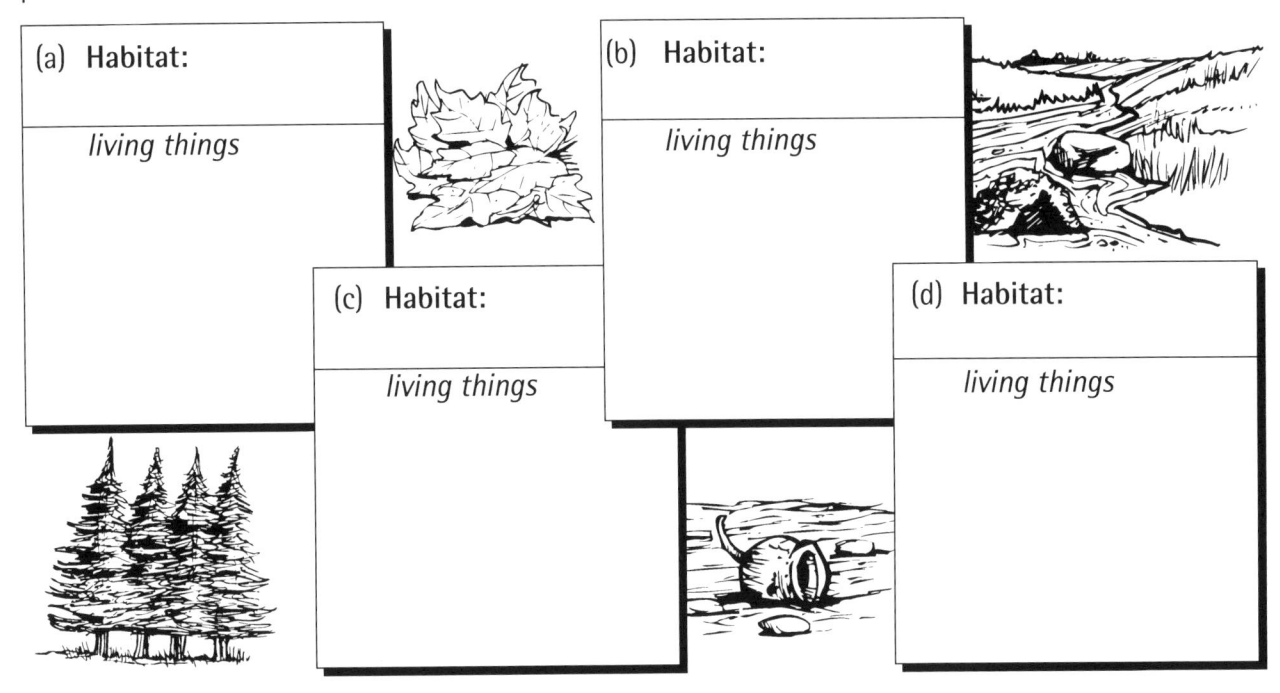

(a) Habitat:
 living things

(b) Habitat:
 living things

(c) Habitat:
 living things

(d) Habitat:
 living things

3. In small groups, discuss how each of the following threats would affect a rainforest and the habitats within it.

habitat loss   **competition with introduced species**   **poaching**   **pollution**

Teachers notes
Threatened species

Lesson outline

- Read together the introduction at the top of the pupil activity page. Encourage the pupils to share their 'quarantine' or airport checking experiences. Discuss why it is important that illegal weapons and drugs are confiscated. Discuss how the introduction of plants and animals may be equally dangerous to us.
- Allow the pupils to independently read the passage about cane toads. Briefly discuss what the positives and negatives were in introducing cane toads to Australia. Question the pupils as to how the cane toad is a threat to wildlife.
- Continue reading the information as a whole class. Encourage the pupils to give other examples of introduced species or species that have become extinct and have caused the ecosystem to become unbalanced.
- Direct the pupils to Question 1. Allow the pupils to work in pairs to discuss and write ways each of the examples could be harmful to ecosystems.
- Allow time for the pupils to share and discuss their suggestions for each example in Question 1.
- Question the pupils as to what they think could be done to solve some of the existing environmental problems stemming from introduced species. Suggest to the pupils that there needs to be laws and incentives in place to encourage people to become careful in their management of introduced species and that governments and politicians are responsible for making these laws.
- As a whole class, brainstorm some of the ways governments are working towards helping the environment. Have the pupils take notes from this discussion to complete Question 2 (a).
- Have the pupils share their ideas with a partner or in a small-group situation. Ask the pupils to record their ideas to complete Question 2 (b).

Answers

1. (a) a herb—may grow too well and choke out existing native species; may be poisonous to native wildlife.
   (b) a small mammal—may be a predator of native wildlife or insects; may carry a disease infecting native wildlife; may have no predators in new environment and multiply to plague proportions.
   (c) an insect—may have no natural predators and multiply to plague proportions; may carry infectious disease; may destroy native vegetation.
   (d) a disease—may infect native wildlife with little or no resistance.
2. (a) Answers will vary
   (b) Answers will vary

Additional activities

- Research the impact these introduced species have had upon the environment: Grey squirrel, North American mink, Japanese knotweed and Canada goose. (For more introduced species, visit http://www.introduced-species.co.uk/).
- Perform a school ground stocktake of introduced and native species. Evaluate whether introduced species have been detrimental to the school's local environment.

Objectives

- Understands the importance of quarantine regulations.
- Understands the impact introduced species have had on the environment.

Curriculum links

Country	Subject	Level	Objectives
England	Science	KS 2	• Know about the different plants and animals found in different habitats.
Northern Ireland	Science and technology	KS 2	• Know about the relationship between animals and plants in a habitat.
Republic of Ireland	Science	5th/6th Class	• Identify the interrelationships and interdependence between plants and animals; e.g. compete with each other.
Scotland	Science	Level E	• Describe examples of competition between plants and between animals.
Wales	Science	KS 2	• Find out about the variety of plants and animals found in different habitats.

Threatened species

Quarantine

Have you ever had to go through 'quarantine' at the airport? This is a system governments have put in place to make sure that dangerous goods such as illegal drugs and weapons can be detected and seized. It is also a place where plants, animals or things which may contain insects or disease are prevented from entering a country. Scientists have found these things can also be dangerous—dangerous to our environment and, in turn, harmful to us.

Cane Toads

There was a terrible problem with cane beetles in Australia. Many farmers were losing their crops. A scientist introduced cane toads from another country to eat the cane beetles. While cane toads did this very well, they have multiplied to plague proportions and are highly toxic to birds and animals, causing a threat to wildlife.

Sometimes, the solution to one problem can cause other problems. An ecosystem is perfectly balanced when we do not touch it. It contains just the right numbers of everything so that all its living things can be sustained. When we introduce something new to an ecosystem it becomes unbalanced and some of the living things within it become threatened. The same thing happens when an element is removed.

1. Describe how you think each of these things could be harmful to our country if they were introduced from another country.

   (a) a herb _____

   _____

   (b) a small mammal _____

   _____

   (c) an insect _____

   _____

   (d) a disease _____

   _____

   > *Scientists and governments work together to help solve environmental problems.*

2. (a) Brainstorm some of the ways governments are working towards helping the environment.

   (b) Brainstorm some other ways you would like to see the government help the environment.

Teachers notes
Conserving Timbertown

Background information

Not everybody likes change; the same can be said for industry and agriculture. People are used to the way things have been done for a very long time and change is nearly always viewed with anxiety—a fear of the unknown. But change is a part of life and is inevitable.

Henry Ford was a man famous for embracing change. He went from an era of horse-drawn carts to wooden automobiles. Ford was clever enough to quickly see that although this was a huge leap forward, it still needed change and modified his invention and built a much lighter metallic chassis. Of course the rest is history, and all over the world today industry and agriculture (including the automobile industry) are facing the inevitable changes required to shift to the sustainability of resources and the reduction/elimination of pollution by-products.

The destruction of forest by the timber industry is a major environmental problem we have been facing for many decades and continues to be a hotly debated topic. The economic importance to towns centred around the industry holds much political sway. Jobs are at stake. Even though the cutting down of old-growth forests is a finite industry and eventually one day that industry will be gone anyway, it is a change that people and politicians find it easier to delay in the short term.

The solution lies in accepting that inevitable change now. It requires the restructuring of how things are done so that sustainability is achieved and pollution is diminished. Industries need to change, but as in the example of the fictitious Timbertown, the changes need not mean an end to the town, nor a dramatic change of lifestyle. With initiative and a willingness to explore alternatives, long-term economic and environmentally-friendly solutions are able to be found.

And as in the case of Timbertown, these were solutions to problems that had to come at some point anyway, as the forest was running out. The ultimate saviour for the town in the long term was to change now and not later, investing in sustainable timber resources, plus expanding into tourism. Had they waited until all the old-growth forest was completely gone, they would have lost the long-term economic benefits of tourism and in so doing would have lost many jobs and maybe even the whole town.

Discussion points

- What kind of opposition do you think you might come up against making the decisions of the conservationist in the story?
- Do you think any of the changes made by the conservationist were unreasonable?
- What other resources could be conserved in a similar manner?
- What towns in your country face a similar predicament to Timbertown?

Websites

http://forests.org/

http://www.panda.org/forest4life/

http://www.amazonteam.org/

Objective

- Reads and understands the role a conservationist plays restructuring the lifestyle of a hypothetical township.

Curriculum links

Country	Subject	Level	Objectives
England	Literacy	Year 5	• Use evidence from a text to explain events or ideas.
		Year 6	• Understand underlying themes, causes and points of view.
Northern Ireland	Language and literacy	KS 2	• Engage in a range of reading activities.
Republic of Ireland	English	5th/6th Class	• Explore non-fiction texts and use comprehension skills.
Scotland	English	Level D	• Complete practical reading tasks.
Wales	English	KS 2	• Read for information.

Conserving Timbertown

Imagine you are a scientist who works at conserving the environment—a 'conservationist'. You have just been employed by a town where the main industry is cutting down trees for timber and producing wood products, like doors and materials to build houses. This town, let's call it 'Timbertown', has always relied on wood from the forest to supply an income to all the townspeople. However, the forest is running out. Furthermore, tourists are now coming to the town to see the remaining tall forest trees, because they are so beautiful and provide a habitat for rare wildlife.

It is your job to ensure that their industry continues in a way that will not further harm the environment. In other words, the townspeople wish to conserve what is left but still keep their jobs. Fortunately, about 10 years ago, the people of Timbertown started a large plantation of timber on disused farm land.

- The first decision you make is that cutting down trees in the natural forest must stop altogether. What is left must be protected in a reserve. This will not only ensure that this precious place is kept for the trees and wildlife living there, but will also ensure an ongoing income for the town from tourists visiting the reserve.

- The second decision you make is to change the industry of logging into harvesting some plantation timber, plus collecting old timber from demolished houses, buildings, old railway sleepers and old electricity poles.

All the loggers still have their jobs, but the jobs have changed a little bit. They take this wood to the carpentry shops where other workers make wood products. Their job has changed as well, because now they are using plantation and recycled timber, but they can still produce the same products.

At the carpentry shop, you find that when they use water in their machinery, it is pumped out of the river and then pumped back into the river when they are finished with it. But it goes back polluted.

- The third decision you make is that all water used in their machinery has to be purified, recycled and used again. No longer are pollutants entering the water.

At the plantation, workers are busily planting more trees for the future. But in the past they have used poisons to kill the wildlife to stop them eating the saplings (young trees).

- The fourth decision you make is to build fences around the plantation. This is a much better solution. It may cost a little more to start with, but you have no ongoing costs with the wildlife eating the saplings in the future.

Timbertown now thrives with incomes from making plantation and recycled timber products, plus an increase in the number of tourists coming to the town. This happened because the forest was protected and the rivers were cleaned up, and poisoning of wildlife at the plantations stopped—the environment actually improved. In fact, an endangered species of owl that had not been seen in Timbertown for over 30 years, had re-established in the forests. What a wonderful job you did as a conservationist! Not only did you manage to keep all the jobs for the residents of Timbertown, you actually increased them. And not only did you manage to conserve what was left of the natural environment of Timbertown, you actually improved the environment.

Teachers notes
Conserving Timbertown

Answers

1. (a) and (c)

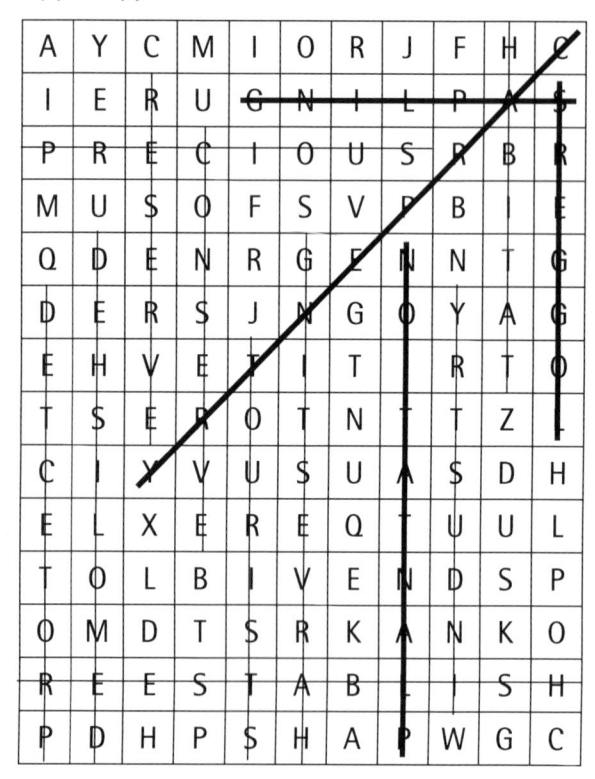

A	Y	C	M	I	O	R	J	F	H	C
I	E	R	U	G	N	I	L	P	A	L
P	R	E	C	I	O	U	S	R	B	R
M	U	S	O	F	S	V	P	B	I	E
Q	D	E	N	R	G	E	N	N	T	G
D	E	R	S	J	G	O	Y	A	G
E	H	V	E	I	T	R	T	O
T	S	E	O	T	N	I	T	Z	I
C	I	Y	V	U	S	U	A	S	D	H
E	L	X	E	R	E	Q	U	U	L
T	O	L	B	I	V	E	N	D	S	P
O	M	D	T	S	R	K	A	N	K	O
R	E	E	S	T	A	B	L	I	S	H
P	D	H	P	S	H	A	P	W	G	C

(b) (i) *conserve*—keep from harm, decay or loss, especially with view to later loss
(ii) *habitat*—natural home of plant or animal
(iii) *re-establish*—return to previous state after lapse or cessation or occurrence of opposite state

(c) (i) plantation
(ii) loggers
(iii) carpentry
(iv) sapling

2. (a) Forests in Timbertown are running out because of over-harvesting and the harvesting of old-growth forests.
(b) Answers will vary.
(c) Stopping logging in natural forests; harvesting plantation timber; recycling water; fencing plantations.

Objectives

- Identifies and understands the meaning of new words.
- Extracts relevant information about conserving Timbertown's lifestyle.

Curriculum links

Country	Subject	Level	Objectives
England	Literacy	Year 5	• Spell words and group words according to their meanings.
		Year 6	• Spell familiar words correctly and employ strategies to spell difficult words.
Northern Ireland	Language and literacy	KS 2	• Acquire and develop a vocabulary.
Republic of Ireland	English	5th/6th Class	• Extend and develop vocabulary and spelling.
Scotland	English	Level D/E	• Know specialist vocabulary from different curricular areas.
Wales	English	KS 2	• Use their knowledge gained from reading to develop their vocabulary.

Conserving Timbertown

1. **Complete these activities.**

    (a) Find each new word in the puzzle.

    New words
    - industry
    - habitat
    - protected
    - precious
    - demolished
    - tourists
    - conserve
    - reserve
    - harvesting
    - re-establish

A	Y	C	M	I	O	R	J	F	H	C
I	E	R	U	G	N	I	L	P	A	S
P	R	E	C	I	O	U	S	R	B	R
M	U	S	O	F	S	V	P	B	I	E
Q	D	E	N	R	G	E	N	N	T	G
D	E	R	S	J	N	G	O	Y	A	G
E	H	V	E	T	I	T	I	R	T	O
T	S	E	R	O	T	N	T	T	Z	L
C	I	Y	V	U	S	U	A	S	D	H
E	L	X	E	R	E	Q	T	U	U	L
T	O	L	B	I	V	E	N	D	S	P
O	M	D	T	S	R	K	A	N	K	O
R	E	E	S	T	A	B	L	I	S	H
P	D	H	P	S	H	A	P	W	G	C

    (b) Write meanings for these words. Use a dictionary to help you.

    (i) conserve _____

    (ii) habitat _____

    (iii) re-establish _____

    (c) There are four extra words associated with logging hidden in the puzzle. Can you find them?

    (i) pl_____
    (ii) l_____
    (iii) c_____
    (iv) s_____

2. **Answer these questions.**

    (a) Why do you think the forests in Timbertown are running out?

    (b) What would your main goals be as a conservationist in Timbertown?

    (i) _____

    (ii) _____

    (c) Describe two improvements you made to Timbertown during your time as a conservationist there.

    (i) _____

    (ii) _____

Prim-Ed Publishing   www.prim-ed.com   The environment   61

Teachers notes
Conserving Timbertown

Lesson outline

- Question the pupils about the air around them. What is it made up of? Is the air we breathe in the same as the air we breathe out? Is the air the same as it was 200 years ago? How is the air cleaned?
- Read together the introductory passage at the top of the pupil activity page. Break up the word 'photosynthesis' into parts to help understand its meaning; i.e. 'photo'—light, 'synthesis'—combining elements into a new form. Encourage the pupils to deduce from this that light, combined with different elements, is changed into a different form, which is energy.
- Direct the pupils to the diagram in Question 1. Read through each of the elements in the box together, describing each and where it comes from. Allow the pupils to reread the introductory paragraph to help them understand and complete the diagram by writing the appropriate element into the correct label.
- Reproduce a diagram for the pupils to view and encourage the pupils to interact in its construction and completion to describe again the process of photosynthesis. Have the pupils check and, if necessary, correct their diagram.
- Read through the passage with blank spaces in Question 2. If the pupils are having trouble understanding photosynthesis, use the diagram as you read the passage to direct them towards the correct answers. Allow the pupils to then complete Question 2 independently.
- Read together the passage which follows on the activity sheet. Clarify any questions the pupils may have about what they have read. In particular, ensure the pupils understand what is being implied by 'tipping the balance scales'.
- Break the class into small groups to discuss ways we could attempt to balance the CO_2 and O_2 levels in our air again. Have each group record their suggestions. After approximately five minutes of discussion time, ask the pupils to rank their suggestions from most important to least important.
- Encourage a spokesperson from each group to share their list in order of rank. Then have the pupils record their own personal 'top three' to complete Question 3.

Answers

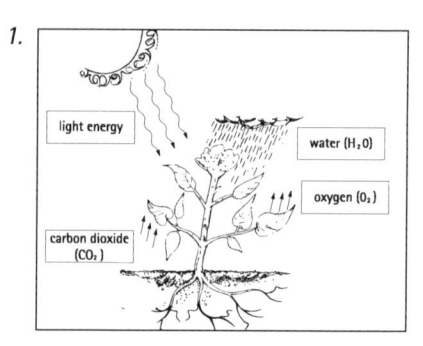

1. [Diagram showing photosynthesis with labels: light energy, water (H_2O), oxygen (O_2), carbon dioxide (CO_2)]

2. Photosynthesis is a process which occurs in green plants which contain chlorophyll. The chlorophyll takes in light energy from the sun to convert carbon dioxide and water into carbohydrates, energy for new growth and the oxygen we need to breathe.

3. Answers will vary.

Additional activities

- Demonstrate transpiration of plants by fastening a plastic bag over several leaves on a bush or tree and leaving overnight. In the morning, water will have collected from the leaves into the plastic bag.
- Look at the chlorophyll-filled cells of a plant under a microscope.

Objectives

- Understands the process of photosynthesis.
- Suggests ways to balance the CO_2 and O_2 levels in the atmosphere.

Curriculum links

Country	Subject	Level	Objectives
England	Science	KS 2	• Know about the effect of light, air, water and temperature on plant growth and the role of the leaf in producing new material for growth.
Northern Ireland	Science and technology	KS 2	• Know about the effect of heat, light and water on plant growth.
Republic of Ireland	Science	5th/6th Class	• Become aware of some of the basic life processes in plants; e.g. use of oxygen and carbon dioxide.
Scotland	Science	Level E	• Identify the raw materials, conditions and products of photosynthesis.
Wales	Science	KS 2	• Know plants need light to produce food for growth and the importance of the leaf in this process.

Conserving Timbertown

Natural air fresheners

Trees, plants and grass are amazing living things. We need them to survive for one very important reason—they clean our air. In fact, they don't just clean it, they transform it from the carbon dioxide we breathe out as waste to the oxygen we need to breathe in. They do this using a process called photosynthesis.

1. Use the chemical symbols or the words in the box to label this diagram showing how photosynthesis works.

Carbon dioxide (CO_2)
Water (H_2O)
Light Energy
Oxygen (O_2)

2. Complete this definition of photosynthesis using words from the box below.

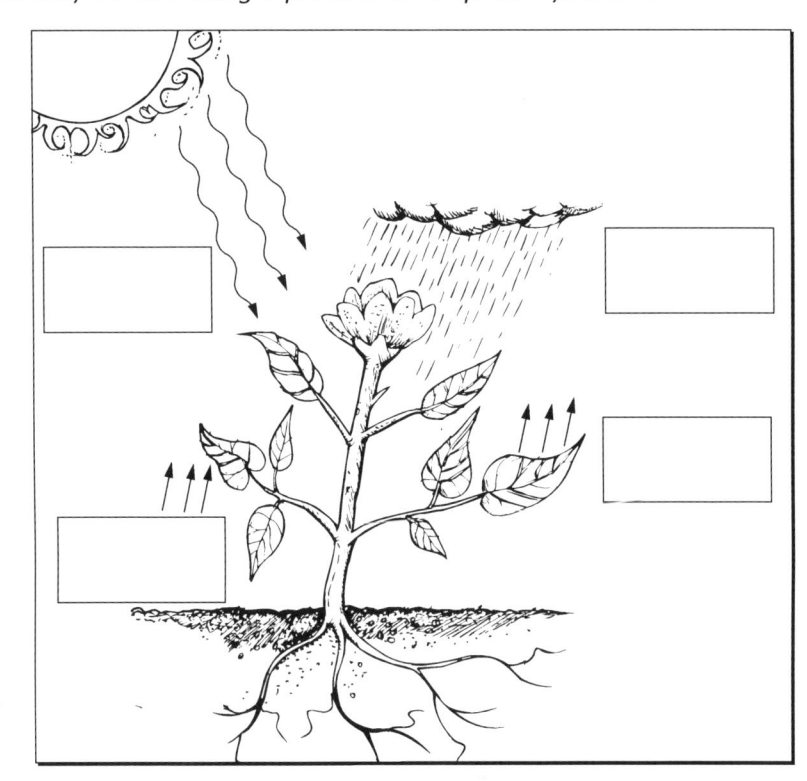

   Photosynthesis is a process which occurs in green plants which contain _____(1).

   The chlorophyll takes in _____(2) _____(3) *from the sun to convert* _____(4) _____(5) *and* _____(6) *into* _____(7), *energy for new growth, and the* _____(8) *we need to breathe.*

carbohydrates	carbon	chlorophyll
dioxide	energy	light
oxygen	water	

Plants have a tough job to do. Not only are we producing CO_2 when we breathe, but we are producing it in the form of pollution from burning fossil fuels to make energy (e.g. every time we use a car). We are beginning to see the balance of CO_2 and O_2 in the air tip towards having too much CO_2.

3. Suggest ways we could attempt to balance the CO_2 and O_2 levels in our air again. Write your top three ideas in the box.

Teachers notes
Conserving Timbertown

Answers

1. Answers will vary
2. Answers will vary
3. Answers will vary

Additional activities

- Research what is made from the trees taken from old-growth forests. Evaluate whether sacrificing old-growth forest trees is justified.
- Write an action plan for how old-growth forests could be preserved without making loggers unemployed.

Lesson outline

- Read together the introductory passage about the consequences of taking action based on two different points of view at the top of the pupil activity page.

- Have the pupils define 'consequence' and explain how one action can lead to a series of further consequences. Encourage the pupils to understand that every argument has two sides and that in most cases, both sides are worthy of consideration.

- Based on the information in the introduction, discuss whether a compromise is possible in this situation. Discuss what is meant by 'win win', 'win lose', and 'lose lose'. Do the pupils think there can be a 'win win' in this situation?

- As a whole class, look at the diagram in Question 1. Describe the diagram so that the pupils can follow how it has been broken down. Explain that this is a 'consequence' chart, designed to predict the consequences of different plans of action. Explain that in both scenarios ('stop logging' and 'continue logging') both the loggers and the environment will be affected somehow.

- Allow the pupils to read through the flow chart of events which form the consequences for loggers if they stop logging.

- Have the pupils work in pairs to predict the consequences of the remaining three categories and write their flow charts accordingly for each.

- Select pupils to share their flow chart for a particular situation. Encourage the class to offer any variations they may have thought of in order to create a fuller picture of the consequences in each situation.

- Based on the consequences understood from answering Question 1, have the pupils decide which outcome is more important and to support their decision with a reason to complete Question 2. Pupils who would like to share their point of view and reasoning should be encouraged to do so.

- Allow the pupils to read and complete Question 3 (a). Refer back to the information on page 59 regarding 'Timbertown'. If the pupils need to reread the passage, allow them to do so.

- Ask the pupils whether they can foresee a resolution to the issue of logging where all parties can be satisfied. Allow them to briefly describe how this might come about to answer 3 (b).

Objectives

- Presents arguments for and against logging of old-growth forests.
- Presents a personal opinion on whether to stop or continue logging.
- Evaluates whether a win/win solution is possible.

Curriculum links

Country	Subject	Level	Objectives
England	Geography	KS 2	• Identify and explain different views that people hold about topical geographical issues.
Northern Ireland	Geography	KS 2	• Know some of the ways people affect/conserve the environment.
Republic of Ireland	Geography/ Science	5th/6th Class	• Identify and discuss a global environmental issue.
Scotland	Health	Level E	• Identify global environmental issues.
Wales	Geography	KS 2	• Recognise that different people have different views about changes made to the environment.

Conserving Timbertown

Consider the consequences

You may have heard about, or seen on the news, people protesting against logging while the loggers sit in their machinery unable to do their job. Both sides of this argument are important.

On one hand, we do need to preserve old-growth forests. On the other hand, the loggers need to be able to do their job so that they can be paid and in turn can feed, clothe and house their families. There are consequences for changing but there are also consequences for continuing in the same way.

1. Write the consequences in each of these situations.

Logging

Stop logging		Continue logging	
Loggers	*Environment*	*Loggers*	*Environment*
Loggers lose their jobs ↓ Have no income ↓ Can't support their family ↓ Lose their house and live on government welfare ↓ Government has to spend money that could have been spent on the environment to support loggers.			

2. Which do you consider is more important?

Loggers keep jobs

Old-growth forests preserved

Why do you think this?

_____
_____
_____
_____

3. (a) Do you think there could be a way for the environment to be preserved and for loggers to keep their jobs?

Yes **No**

(b) Suggest how you could solve the problem.

_____
_____
_____
_____

Teachers notes
Is it a whale or a shark?

Background information

The whale shark (Rhincodon typus) is very much the world's largest fish and although it is a shark, it's not your typical flesh-eating type. It is a gentle plankton-eating filter-feeder, and in its search for food is highly migratory, making it difficult to study. It has beautiful colouration; dark grey to a reddish or greenish brown on the back and sides, and is spotted with a white or yellowish series of spots, smallest and fewest on the head.

This combination of characteristics makes this fish a highly desirable animal-watching experience and over the past five years a significant ecotourism industry has evolved at Ningaloo Marine Park. Western Australia is the only place known in the world where whale sharks visit on a regular basis—March to April each year. But why mostly immature males visit is one of the many mysteries this elusive creature retains.

Even though the meat of the whale shark is not highly sought after, it is still fished for its oil-rich liver. Taiwan is the biggest consumer with India, Pakistan, China and the Maldives contributing to the catch. Unfortunately there has been a recent increase in the demand for shark-fin soup, which leads to a cruel fishing practice where the fin is taken and often the shark thrown back and left to die. This may further threaten the whale shark.

In Australian waters the whale shark is fully protected. However, it is an extremely shy animal and can be adversely affected if disturbed. For this reason, CALM (the Department of Conservation and Land Management) in Western Australia has regulations surrounding whale shark watching. These include:

- Boats must observe a 50-metre radius 'contact zone' around whale sharks. Only one vessel at a time may operate in a contact zone, for a period not exceeding 90 minutes, and during that time must stay at least 30 metres from the shark.
- If a second vessel arrives at the contact zone, it must stand off at least 250 metres. Any further vessels must stay at least 400 metres away from the shark.
- People swimming with whale sharks must not touch or ride on the animal. Swimmers must stay one metre clear of the shark's head or body, and four metres away from its tail flukes.

Obviously there are both intrinsic and economic (via tourism) reasons for conserving whale sharks. What could be of even further significance are the reports of this animal's strong anti-tumour activity in its liver (Note: not yet scientifically researched). Other sharks may also have similar qualities. Once again the natural world reveals another clue to finding the answers to some of humanity's distressing afflictions, such as cancer.

Discussion points

- Is a whale shark a shark or a whale? Why? What scientific evidence could you use to support your belief?
- Why do you think that the whale shark is a largely unexplored creature? What benefits do you foresee may arise from researching the whale shark?
- How has over-fishing affected whale sharks?

Websites

http://www.fish.wa.gov.au/rec/broc/fishcard/whaleshk.html
(Ningaloo Reef)

http://www.new-brunswick.net/new-brunswick/sharks/species/whale.html
(good pictures)

Objective

- Reads and understands informational text about the whale shark.

Curriculum links

Country	Subject	Level	Objectives
England	Literacy	Year 5	• Use evidence from a text to explain events or ideas.
		Year 6	• Understand underlying themes, causes and points of view.
Northern Ireland	Language and literacy	KS 2	• Engage in a range of reading activities.
Republic of Ireland	English	5th/6th Class	• Explore non-fiction texts and use comprehension skills.
Scotland	English	Level D	• Complete practical reading tasks.
Wales	English	KS 2	• Read for information.

Is it a whale or a shark?

When is a whale a whale and a shark a shark? As you know, whales are mammals, and even though they live in the ocean, they still give birth to live young, suckle their young on milk and are ectothermic (warm-blooded). However, sharks are actually fish, are endothermic (cold-blooded) and usually do not care for their young.

So are whale sharks mammals or fish? Let's have a closer look.

- Whale sharks eat plankton by filter feeding.
- No-one really knows how they have their babies, but we think the young develop in their egg cases inside the mother's body and the babies are born live.

These two facts look like they could be whales, because some whales eat plankton by filter feeding and they give live birth. However, on further examination:

- whalesharks have gills,
- they are cold-blooded,
- and, once their babies are born they are on their own, not needing milk from their mother.

Yes, indeed, whale sharks are very much fish—in fact by far the largest fish in the world. They are the size of a whale, up to 12 metres in length and weighing over 20 tonnes. They are extraordinary creatures—both beautiful and gentle—and also completely harmless, unlike many other sharks. This is because they only eat plankton (microscopic plants and animals) and therefore are not carnivorous or dangerous.

Numbers of whale sharks are declining and are under threat from overfishing. However, hardly any scientists in the world have ever studied them, and very little is known about their habits. Their current World Conservation Union (ICUN) status is 'data deficient'.

Even though we have lots to learn about whale sharks, conservation of the species is already underway. This is for some very good reasons.

1. Whale sharks are an ecotourism resource, such as practised at Ningaloo Reef in Western Australia.

2. Their liver is reported to have a strong anti-tumour activity, which may help scientists in their fight for a cure for cancer.

3. Whale sharks are one of the ocean's most secretive and amazing creatures— gentle giants that deserve all the protection we can give them.

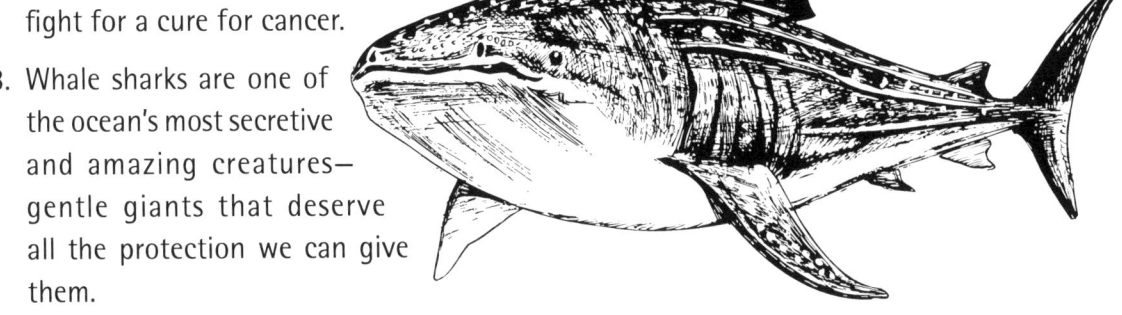

Teachers notes
Is it a whale or a shark?

Answers

1. (a) and (c)

D	M	I	C	R	O	S	C	O	P	I	C	T
E	C	T	O	T	H	E	R	M	I	C	A	S
F	P	D	H	P	T	N	Y	U	M	I	E	U
I	L	M	X	M	O	D	P	I	U	Q	H	O
C	A	E	N	I	T	O	N	N	E	S	A	R
I	N	T	I	Y	R	T	P	S	I	T	R	O
E	K	R	F	I	S	H	A	I	R	P	M	V
N	T	E	S	O	Y	E	P	M	S	R	L	I
T	O	S	S	E	C	R	E	T	I	V	E	N
A	N	T	I	T	U	M	O	U	R	R	S	R
M	A	M	M	A	L	I	R	Z	V	N	S	A
C	G	K	O	S	W	C	I	P	J	F	B	C

   (b) (i) endothermic—cold-blooded

       (ii) ectothermic—warm-blooded

       (iii) plankton—drifting or floating microscopic forms of organic life

   (c) (1) fish

       (2) metres

       (3) tonnes

2. (a) A whale shark is a shark because it has gills, is cold-blooded, its young are born from eggs and do not feed from their mother.

   (b) The status of whale sharks is 'data deficient' because there are very few whale sharks remaining in the wild to research, they are very shy creatures, and they cannot be successfully held in captivity.

   (c) As an ecotourism resource; for their strong 'anti-tumour' potential; because they are unique.

Objective

- Identifies and understands the meaning of new words.

Curriculum links

Country	Subject	Level	Objectives
England	Literacy	Year 5	• Spell words and group words according to their meanings.
		Year 6	• Spell familiar words correctly and employ strategies to spell difficult words.
Northern Ireland	Language and literacy	KS 2	• Acquire and develop a vocabulary.
Republic of Ireland	English	5th/6th Class	• Extend and develop vocabulary and spelling.
Scotland	English	Level D/E	• Know specialist vocabulary from different curricular areas.
Wales	English	KS 2	• Use their knowledge gained from reading to develop their vocabulary.

Is it a whale or a shark?

1. **Complete these activities.**

   (a) Find each new word in the puzzle.

   New words
   - endothermic
   - mammal
   - harmless
   - microscopic
   - anti-tumour
   - ectothermic
   - plankton
   - carnivorous
   - deficient
   - secretive

D	M	I	C	R	O	S	C	O	P	I	C	T
E	C	T	O	T	H	E	R	M	I	C	A	S
F	P	D	H	P	T	N	Y	U	M	I	E	U
I	L	M	X	M	O	D	P	I	U	Q	H	O
C	A	E	N	I	T	O	N	N	E	S	A	R
I	N	T	I	Y	R	T	P	S	I	T	R	O
E	K	R	F	I	S	H	A	I	R	P	M	V
N	T	E	S	O	Y	E	P	M	S	R	L	I
T	O	S	S	E	C	R	E	T	I	V	E	N
A	N	T	I	T	U	M	O	U	R	R	S	R
M	A	M	M	A	L	I	R	Z	V	N	S	A
C	G	K	O	S	W	C	I	P	J	F	B	C

   (b) Write meanings for these words. Use a dictionary to help you.

   (i) endothermic _____

   (ii) ectothermic _____

   (iii) plankton _____

   (c) Complete this sentence and find the three missing words in the puzzle above.

   > The whale shark is the largest _____(1) in the world. It grows up to 12 _____(2) long and can weigh over 20 _____(3).

2. **Answer these questions.**

   (a) Is a whale shark a shark or a whale?

   | whale | shark |

   List reasons why. _____
   _____
   _____
   _____

   (b) Why do you think the status of whale sharks is 'data deficient'?
   _____
   _____
   _____

   (c) Give three reasons why whale sharks should be conserved.

   (i) _____

   (ii) _____

   (iii) _____

Prim-Ed Publishing   www.prim-ed.com   **The environment**   69

Teachers notes
Is it a whale or a shark?

Answers

1. (a) Data deficient
   (b) The status of whale sharks is data deficient because there are very few whale sharks remaining in the wild to research, they are very shy creatures, and they cannot be successfully held in captivity.
2. (a) extinct
   (b) least concern
   (c) critically endangered
3. Answers will vary

Additional activities

- Visit a zoo or local wildlife park. Identify creatures which are endangered. Choose an endangered species you have seen to research and find out why it is valuable to the environment.
- Brainstorm a list of native animals. Use the Wildlife Status categories to categorise them.

Lesson outline

- Discuss endangered species. Ask the pupils how they think people decide whether a species is threatened and who is responsible for defining and updating the status of different species in the world.
- Direct the pupils to the status categories on the pupil activity page. Discuss the kinds of information that would be required about an animal to be able to use this chart.
- Allow the pupils to read independently the introductory passage at the top of the pupil activity page.
- Provide each pupil with a copy of page 67. Have them read the page and highlight the information giving the status of whale sharks. They can then transfer this information to complete Question 1 (a).
- Brainstorm a list of reasons why the whale shark might be difficult to gain data about. Direct the pupils to use these ideas to assist them in completing 1 (b).
- Read together Question 2, including the information about the Tasmanian tiger given in part (a). As a whole class, deduce what category the Tasmanian tiger might be in, based on the information given. Guide the pupils through the elimination process in order to narrow down the possibilities.
- Discuss the difficulty in arriving at an absolute decision about an animal being extinct. Argue what would need to happen for us to be convinced of an animal's extinction.
- Allow the pupils to apply the same process to parts (b) and (c).
- As a whole class, apply the process to human beings to determine their status. Have the pupils write reasons for why humans are not under threat or for why they may inadvertently be under threat.
- Encourage the pupils to share their thoughts on the status of humans with the class.

Objectives

- Recognises why whale sharks are in the 'data deficient' category of wildlife status.
- Identifies the status of a variety of animals.

Curriculum links

Country	Subject	Level	Objectives
England	Science	KS 2	• Use keys.
Northern Ireland	Science and technology	KS 2	• Examine data from the world around them.
Republic of Ireland	Science	5th/6th Class	• Sort data.
Scotland	Science	Level C	• Give examples of living things that are rare or extinct.
Wales	Science	KS 2	• Use keys.

Is it a whale or a shark?

The status of wildlife

The IUCN (World Conservation Union) has created status categories to determine how threatened a species of animal is so that the most effective steps can be taken to conserve that animal and its environment.

1. (a) Look at the IUCN Wildlife Status Categories in the table below. Read the passage on page 67 to find out the status of whale sharks.

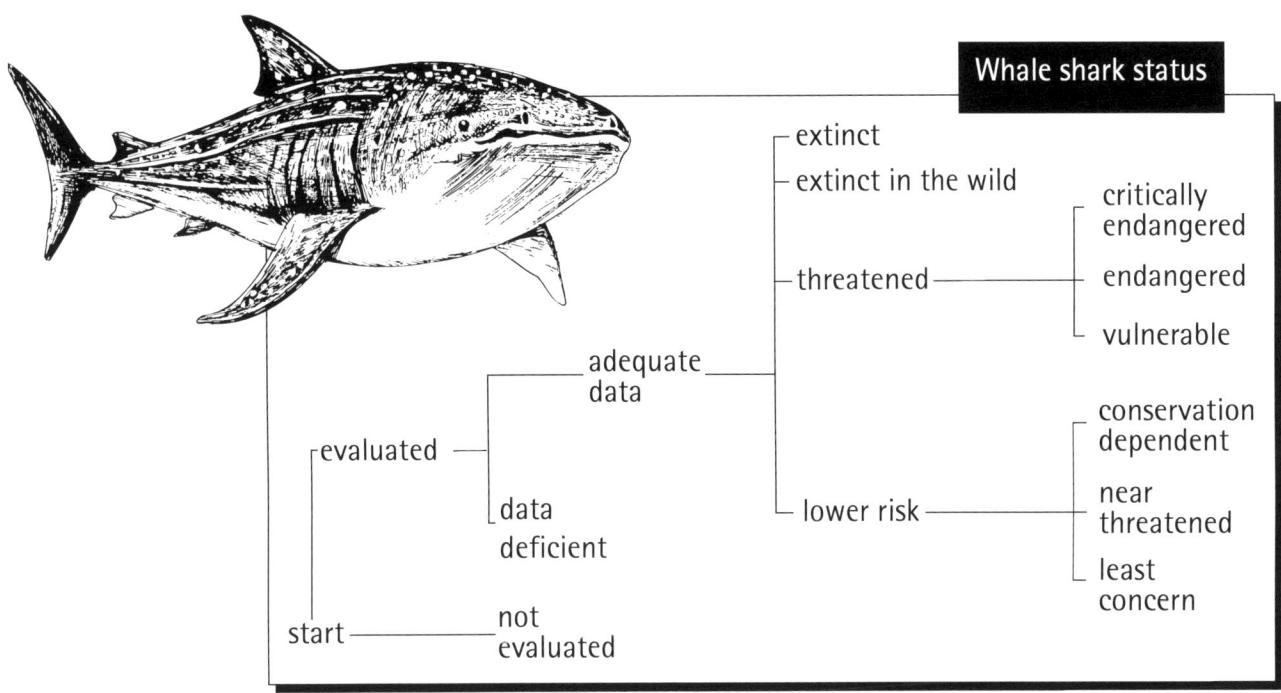

Whale shark status

```
                                            ┌─ extinct
                                            ├─ extinct in the wild
                                            │                    ┌─ critically endangered
                            ┌─ adequate ────┼─ threatened ───────┼─ endangered
                            │   data        │                    └─ vulnerable
              ┌─ evaluated ─┤                │                    ┌─ conservation dependent
              │             │                └─ lower risk ───────┼─ near threatened
              │             └─ data deficient                     └─ least concern
  start ──────┤
              └─ not evaluated
```

(b) Describe why whale sharks are in this category. _____

_____

2. Read the information and use the diagram above to determine the status of the following animals.

   (a) The Tasmanian tiger has not been seen in the wild for over 50 years. There are none in captivity.

   Status

   (b) Red kangaroos are plentiful. Their habitat is not threatened.

   Status

   (c) There are only 110 Northern hairy-nosed wombats remaining. Their situation is critical.

   Status

3. What do you think is the status of humans?

   _____

   Why do you think this?

   _____
   _____
   _____
   _____

Teachers notes
Is it a whale or a shark?

Lesson outline

- Ask the pupils to share scary experiences they have had. Discuss how they felt.
- Read together the information at the top of the pupil activity page. Question the pupils as to whether they would be prepared to swim with normal sharks. Ask how swimming with whale sharks might be different.
- Imagine the size of a whale shark. Have the pupils step out the length of a long wheelbase four-wheel drive. In the playground, step out this length 10 times end to end to show the length of a whale shark.
- Read together Question 1 and allow the pupils to write what they imagine would be the reasons for tourists wanting to swim with whale sharks.
- Have the pupils close their eyes and imagine they are swimming with whale sharks. If possible, play music or sound effects to enhance the pupils' feeling of being underwater with these gentle giants. Encourage the pupils to think about the experience through each of their senses.
- Direct the pupils to complete Question 2 (a) and (b) to describe their imagined experience of swimming with whale sharks.
- Read together the information which follows on the pupil activity page about rules for swimming with whale sharks. Choose individual pupils to read out the rules.
- Discuss the importance of rules and why they are necessary. Discuss how such rules might be monitored and what might happen if they are not kept.
- Allow the pupils to complete Question 3, addressing each of the rules stated for swimming with whale sharks.

Answers

1. Answers will vary
2. (a) Answers will vary
   (b) Teacher check
3. Answers will vary

Additional activities

- Write a descriptive narrative of an imagined adventure swimming with whale sharks.
- Have the pupils imagine they are a little known sea creature. Ask them to describe their characteristics and write rules for how they would want to be treated by tourists coming to swim with them.

Objective

- Identifies and considers the rules for people swimming with whale sharks.

Curriculum links

Country	Subject	Level	Objectives
England	Geography	KS 2	• Recognise how people can improve the environment.
Northern Ireland	Geography	KS 2	• Know some of the ways in which people conserve the environment globally.
Republic of Ireland	Geography/Science	5th/6th Class	• Come to appreciate individual, community and national responsibility for environmental care.
Scotland	Science	Level C	• Explain how living things and the environment can be protected.
Wales	Geography	KS 2	• Understand the individual's responsibility for the environment.

Is it a whale or a shark?

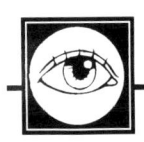

Swimming with whale sharks

Have you ever considered swimming with sharks? Perhaps you don't like the idea! What if you knew they were harmless? Many people have swum with whale sharks—the size of 10 big four-wheel drives—and have described it as the most exhilarating thing they have experienced!

1. Why do you think hundreds of tourists line up each year for their chance to swim with whale sharks?

___

2. (a) Describe what swimming with whale sharks might be like.

   (b) Draw yourself swimming alongside this fully grown whale shark. Don't forget to keep yourself in proportion.

Rules

- People swimming with whale sharks must not touch or ride on the animal.
- Swimmers must stay one metre clear of the shark's head or body, and four metres from its tail flukes.
- Boats must stay at least 50 metres away from whale sharks.

When swimming with whale sharks, there are rules which must be followed.

Australian waters are fully protected and can therefore be monitored to ensure these rules are kept.

3. Why do you think these specific rules have been made?

___

Prim-Ed Publishing www.prim-ed.com **The environment** 73

Teachers notes
Natural ecosystems

Background information

One of the aspects of biodiversity is ecosystem diversity. The world has hundreds of different ecosystems. This means that there is a great diversity among the types of ecosystems found here. Within each ecosystem is a plethora of different habitats, each supporting its own unique wildlife.

Ecosystems are just as diverse and important in aquatic environments. In fact, ocean ecosystems are actually richer in diversity than the most diverse terrestrial ecosystems, rainforests. What is important to understand is that it is easier for governments and people to want to save rainforests and reefs because they are beautiful places. Mangroves and deserts may not be as appealing, but as ecosystems they have just as much value, because the life supported there is so vastly different from that supported by others.

Conservationists take a holistic approach to environmental management, because species survival cannot be attained sustainably in isolation. Some threatened species, although not extinct, only remain alive in captive situations. For such a species to be re-introduced and allowed to naturally re-establish, the whole ecosystem needs to be in a healthy condition.

The worst scenario for this type of recovery is when a species has become extinct in the wild. Many conservationists now take a more proactive approach to species management, working to attain ecosystem protection for groups of plants and animals in a region while population numbers are still relatively good. Prevention is always better than cure, particularly when we are talking about environmental management, because once disturbed it is unlikely an area can regenerate completely to its original state.

Discussion points

- What constitutes an ecosystem?
- Why is it important to protect whole ecosystems rather than just a particular species?

Websites

http://www.ecokidsonline.com/pub/index.cfm
http://www.mbgnet.net/
http://passporttoknowledge.com/rainforest/main.html

Objective

- Reads and understands informational text about protecting a wide range of natural ecosystems.

Curriculum links

Country	Subject	Level	Objectives
England	Literacy	Year 5	• Use evidence from a text to explain events or ideas.
		Year 6	• Understand underlying themes, causes and points of view.
Northern Ireland	Language and literacy	KS 2	• Engage in a range of reading activities.
Republic of Ireland	English	5th/6th Class	• Explore non-fiction texts and use comprehension skills.
Scotland	English	Level D	• Complete practical reading tasks.
Wales	English	KS 2	• Read for information.

Natural ecosystems

Forests provide a home to two-thirds of all terrestrial (land) species in the world. Therefore, forests are very diverse ecosystems. An ecosystem is a community of different species interacting with one another and with the non-living environment. So often when we think about what would be a good area to protect in a National Park, we think about rainforests and forests.

But of course, forests are not the only type of ecosystem. Other ecosystems include:

- Arid areas (dry, desert)
- Mangroves
- Oceans
- Reefs
- Grasslands
- Wetlands
- Islands
- Coastal areas
- Heathlands
- Alpine areas

All these ecosystems have their own characteristics with their own types of plants and animals. Take for example an arid area. What do you immediately think of? Desert with dry sand? Amazingly, however, arid areas have a diverse range of habitats, just like rainforests. A habitat is a place where an animal can live—its home. These habitats include:

- Spinifex (tough grassy plants)
- Dunes
- Scrub
- Cliffs
- Gorges
- Dry riverbeds
- Waterholes

So within even the harshest of ecosystems, there are a number of habitats that can support different kinds of animals.

Many of these arid species are very different from those found in forests, so when we are deciding on what areas should become protected in National Parks and reserves, we need to save all different types of ecosystems.

Think of some of the major National Parks in the world. There are rainforests protected in the Amazon National Park in Brazil, arid areas protected in the Arches National Park in the USA, reefs protected in the Great Barrier Reef Marine Park in Australia and mountain areas protected in the Kilimanjaro National Park in Tanzania.

When it is realised that a species has become threatened and there are not many of that plant or animal left, an action plan is devised to try to save that individual species from becoming extinct. Recently, conservationists have started to look at finding ways to help all the threatened species in an ecosystem, rather than just concentrating on one. Often what threatens one animal or plant species threatens many others too.

Because so much of the world is now being used to support the needs of humans, more than ever we need to protect all kinds of different ecosystems.

Teachers notes
Natural ecosystems

Answers

1. (a) and (c)

I	N	T	E	R	A	C	T	I	N	G	P	I	F	B
A	E	K	R	E	H	V	P	A	N	A	L	J	G	L
S	M	R	I	H	A	J	R	F	U	I	A	K	O	X
Z	W	A	T	E	R	H	O	L	E	S	I	E	R	W
M	A	P	U	S	S	E	T	U	W	X	R	S	G	B
E	Z	Q	F	H	U	E	B	O	E	T	D	E	C	
T	M	A	R	F	S	N	C	H	E	S	S	E	S	G
S	T	N	G	I	E	T	T	O	S	I	E	B	D	M
Y	D	O	S	L	N	E	E	J	R	N	R	R	B	P
S	L	I	X	C	U	E	Q	L	E	I	R	E	U	K
O	F	T	R	D	D	Y	U	N	V	V	P	E	V	R	G
C	H	A	R	A	C	T	E	R	I	S	T	I	C	S
E	D	N	H	L	R	E	O	Y	D	K	P	R	S	C

(b) (i) terrestrial—of land opposite to water; living on the ground, growing in the soil
(ii) arid—dry, parched, too dry to support vegetation
(iii) alpine—of the alps or any lofty mountains

(c) (i) spinifex (ii) dunes (iii) scrub (iv) cliffs
(v) gorges (vi) riverbeds (vii) waterholes

2. (a) (i) An ecosystem is a community of different species interacting with one another and with the non-living environment.
(ii) A habitat is a place where an animal can live. There are many habitats within one ecosystem.
(b) Ecosystems can be different from one another in vegetation, climate, animals and topography.
(c) Examples may vary if not chosen from the text.
(i) The Great Barrier Reef Marine Park, Australia
(ii) Kilimanjaro National Park, Tanzania
(iii) Amazon National Park, Brazil
(iv) Arches National Park, USA

Objectives
- Identifies and understands the meaning of new words.
- Extracts relevant information about natural ecosystems.

Curriculum links

Country	Subject	Level	Objectives
England	Literacy	Year 5	• Spell words and group words according to their meanings.
		Year 6	• Spell familiar words correctly and employ strategies to spell difficult words.
Northern Ireland	Language and literacy	KS 2	• Acquire and develop a vocabulary.
Republic of Ireland	English	5th/6th Class	• Extend and develop vocabulary and spelling.
Scotland	English	Level D/E	• Know specialist vocabulary from different curricular areas.
Wales	English	KS 2	• Use their knowledge gained from reading to develop their vocabulary.

Natural ecosystems

1. **Complete these activities.**

   (a) Find each new word in the puzzle.

   New words
   - terrestrial
   - ecosystem
   - national park
   - arid
   - alpine
   - diverse
   - interacting
   - characteristics
   - harsh
   - protect

I	N	T	E	R	A	C	T	I	N	G	P	I	F	B
A	E	K	R	E	H	V	P	A	N	A	L	J	G	L
S	M	R	I	H	A	J	R	F	U	I	A	K	O	X
Z	W	A	T	E	R	H	O	L	E	S	I	E	R	W
M	A	P	U	S	S	E	T	U	W	X	R	S	G	B
E	Z	L	Q	F	H	U	E	B	O	E	T	D	E	C
T	M	A	P	F	S	N	C	H	E	F	S	E	S	G
S	T	N	G	I	E	T	T	O	S	I	E	B	D	M
Y	D	O	S	L	N	E	E	J	R	N	R	R	B	P
S	L	I	X	C	U	E	Q	L	E	I	R	E	U	K
O	F	T	R	D	D	Y	U	N	V	P	E	V	R	G
C	H	A	R	A	C	T	E	R	I	S	T	I	C	S
E	D	N	H	L	R	E	O	Y	D	K	P	R	S	C

   (b) Write meanings for these words. Use a dictionary to help you.

   (i) terrestrial _____

   (ii) arid _____

   (iii) alpine _____

   (c) There are seven extra words hidden in the puzzle which describe habitats found in a desert. Can you find them?

   (i) sp_____
   (ii) d_____
   (iii) s_____
   (iv) cl_____
   (v) g_____
   (vi) dry r_____
   (vii) w_____

2. **Answer these questions.**

   (a) (i) What is an ecosystem?

   (ii) What is a habitat?

   (b) List ways in which ecosystems can be different from one another.

   (c) Name a National Park which protects each of the following systems.

   (i) reef _____
   (ii) alpine areas _____
   (iii) rainforest _____
   (iv) arid area _____

Teachers notes
Natural ecosystems

Answers

1. prickly pear – desert, bulbs – alpine, mangrove tree – mangrove, staghorn – rainforest
2. Answers will vary
3. Answers will vary

Additional activities

- Brainstorm a list of ecosystems. Use an atlas to identify National Parks or reserves which protect these ecosystems. Evaluate which ecosystems may be under the greatest threats.
- Visit a National Park and investigate the ecosystem it protects.

Lesson outline

- Revise the difference between an ecosystem and a habitat. If possible, provide a variety of different plant types for the pupils to view and decide what kind of ecosystem they may have come from.

- Read together the information at the top of the pupil activity page. Clarify what is meant by 'climate' and 'topography' by having the pupils describe the climate and topography of their own ecosystem.

- Direct the pupils to the pictures in Question 1. Look at each plant type. Observe their characteristics and deduce what kind of climate and topography might suit each. Allow the pupils to use the information from this discussion to complete Question 1 by matching each plant to an ecosystem and then describing the unique requirements provided for the plant by the ecosystem. For example, mangroves require salt water moving around their exposed roots to grow successfully.

- Allow time for the pupils to share their deductions about the ways each ecosystem provides for its related plants.

- Encourage the pupils to share experiences they have had visiting National Parks. Brainstorm a class list of National Parks visited by members of the class.

- Have the pupils use this class list to complete Question 2.

- Have the pupils read independently Question 3 (a), (b) and (c). Allow them to write their experiences to complete the question.

- If time permits, have the pupils draw a picture or diagram of what they would expect to find in the National Park they have chosen to visit. Have the pupils add descriptive captions to annotate their drawings. The artwork can then be displayed and discussed informally among the pupils.

Objectives

- Identifies and explains why particular plants belong to a particular ecosystem.
- Describes the vegetation, climate and topography of a specific National Park.

Curriculum links

Country	Subject	Level	Objectives
England	Science	KS 2	Know about the different plants found in different habitats.
Northern Ireland	Science and technology	KS 2	Know about the plants in a habitat.
Republic of Ireland	Science	5th/6th Class	Recognise that there is a great diversity of plants in different regions and environments.
Scotland	Science	Level D	Give examples of how plants are suited to their environment.
Wales	Science	KS 2	Find out about the variety of plants found in different habitats.

Natural ecosystems

Special plants of special places

Plant life or vegetation provides the habitats to support a wider community of living things. The types of plants that grow in an ecosystem depends on the climate (rainfall, temperature, humidity, sunshine), the type of soil and the shape of the land (topography).

1. Match each of these plants to the ecosystem you think you would most likely find it. Give reasons for your answers in the spaces provided.

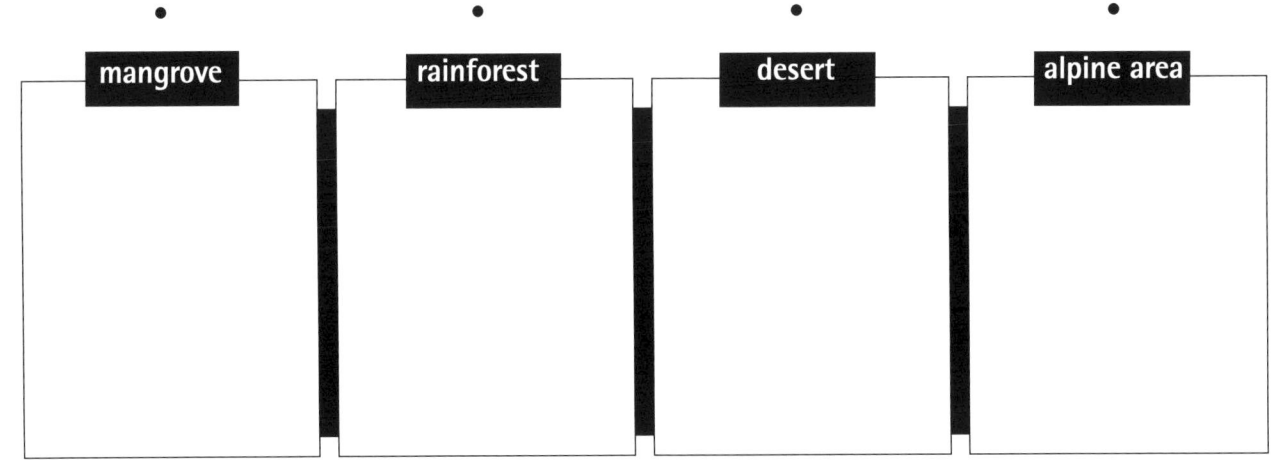

mangrove	rainforest	desert	alpine area

2. Brainstorm the National Parks you know of in your country. List them in the box.

3. (a) Which of these National Parks have you visited?

   (b) Which would you most like to visit?

   (c) Briefly describe the vegetation, climate and topography you expect to find when you visit this National Park.

Teachers notes
Natural ecosystems

Lesson outline

- Provide the pupils with pupil atlases. Have them look at the different types of maps of Australia, including topographic, rainfall and vegetation. Discuss how these elements combine to produce different ecosystems across Australia.

- Look at the map on the pupil activity page. The pupils should be encouraged to compare vegetation categories on the vegetation map in the atlas to those provided on the activity sheet.

- Have the pupils colour the map using the colours given to become familiar with the location of different ecosystems within Australia.

- Discuss the location of any ecosystems which may have surprised the pupils and what they would have expected to find there instead.

- Compare the map of the ecosystem (vegetation) to the topographic map in the atlas. Do the alpine areas match the mountains on the topographic map?

- Compare the map of ecosystems to the rainfall map. Are the rainforests found in the areas of highest rainfall?

- Encourage the pupils to identify other similarities and differences among the different types of maps in the atlas. The pupils should be given ample time to investigate these matters independently.

Answers

1. Teacher check

Additional activities

- Use a dictionary or encyclopaedia to define each of the ecosystems listed in the table. Attempt to recall places you have visited which match some of the ecosystems listed.

- Choose an ecosystem to describe expressively and illustrate. Include reference to its beauty and value.

Objective

- Identifies major ecosystems found in Australia on a map.

Curriculum links

Country	Subject	Level	Objectives
England	Geography	KS 2	• Use atlases and maps.
Northern Ireland	Geography	KS 2	• Locate places studied in atlases and maps.
Republic of Ireland	Geography	5th/6th Class	• Engage in practical use of maps.
Scotland	Society	Level D	• Describe the main features of maps.
Wales	Geography	KS 2	• Use maps and identify and locate places using atlases.

Natural ecosystems

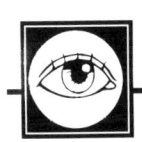

Australia's ecosystems

1. Use the information in the table to colour the major ecosystems found in Australia.

rainforests	1	red
eucalypt forests	2	dark green
scrub	3	yellow
woodlands	4	light green
alpine areas (mountain moor)	5	purple
reef	6	pink
grasslands	7	light blue
heathlands	8	dark blue
saltbush	9	grey
desert	10	orange

Teachers notes
Look at us now!

Background information

Many zoos are committed to conserving the world's threatened species through education, research, breeding programmes, reintroduction programmes and fundraising to support those programmes.

The chance that many people will see elephants, seals, rock wallabies and iguanas in the wild are few. If we are lucky we will be fortunate to enjoy wild experiences at some time, but few will live a David Attenborough life. Thanks to people such as David we are privy to the lifestyles of many of these exotic animals via the media, and although this has enhanced our understanding of the natural world, nothing can replace the experience of living it.

Through the living exhibit of plants in botanical gardens and animals in zoos we are afforded a glimpse into the natural world. Many zoos now encourage a more involved experience that connects people with animals and plants. They encourage extension outside of simply visiting, by motivating people to become actively involved in conservation.

All this has and is still being achieved by leaving behind the outdated ideas of using animals for entertainment and becoming innovative to create a **learning** experience that is not only enjoyable, but also inspiring and challenging.

Discussion points

- Why shouldn't animals be used to entertain the public?
- If zoos are not to entertain people, why do they need to exist?

Websites

http://www.edinburghzoo.org.uk
http://www.dublinzoo.ie
http://www.bristolzoo.org.uk
http://www.wmsp.co.uk
http://www.woburnsafari.co.uk
http://www.sealsanctuary.co.uk/hunt1.html
http://www.sealsanctuary.co.uk/oban1.co.uk

Objective

- Reads and understands the roles modern zoos and wildlife parks play.

Curriculum links

Country	Subject	Level	Objectives
England	Literacy	Year 5	• Use evidence from a text to explain events or ideas.
		Year 6	• Understand underlying themes, causes and points of view.
Northern Ireland	Language and literacy	KS 2	• Engage in a range of reading activities.
Republic of Ireland	English	5th/6th Class	• Explore non-fiction texts and use comprehension skills.
Scotland	English	Level D	• Complete practical reading tasks.
Wales	English	KS 2	• Read for information.

Look at us now!

For many years now, zoos and aquariums have used animals to entertain us by getting them to perform 'tricks'. However, this teaches us nothing about their natural behaviour. Today, animals in captivity are usually provided with stimulating activities, allowing visitors to observe more natural behaviour. Visitors enjoy themselves and feel a sense of wonderment at being able to see such amazing animals up close. They also go away having learnt something.

Many of our threatened species live in places a long way from where we do. And even if we visit those places, the animals are so rare that we probably won't even see one. Zoos provide a place to showcase threatened animals so that we can see what they look like and learn about them. Zoos also provide scientists with a way to gain a better understanding of the animals' living needs, such as habitat, diet and how they reproduce and raise their young. In the same way as zoos, botanical gardens provide an opportunity to see and learn about threatened plants.

At sea life sanctuaries, many of the animals on display have been orphaned or injured. The vets at the sanctuaries will often work through the night to help sick sea creatures. Once the animals are a healthy weight and free from wounds or infection they are transferred to an outdoor pool to gain the strength they will need when they are finally returned to the sea. Not only do these sanctuaries provide medical treatment for these creatures, they also educate visitors on the problems faced by sea wildlife.

At safari parks, breeding programmes are carried out in free-range environments—a bit like 'Jurassic Park'. Visitors travel in a car or bus and gates open and close electronically as they move through one huge paddock to another. The areas for animals to live in are so large that it's hard to imagine they are actually in captivity. This is the best way to see animals at zoos. It gives visitors the feeling that they are in the wild with the animals, a part of their environment, instead of the animals being in cages as part of our environment. Some of the animals have bred to such large numbers that zookeepers have been able to release some back into the wild.

Today, zoos do very important work. Some care for injured wildlife, some breed animals to be released back into the wild and all zoos teach us about the importance of understanding animals before we can begin to help them.

Teachers notes
Look at us now!

Answers

1. (a) and (c)

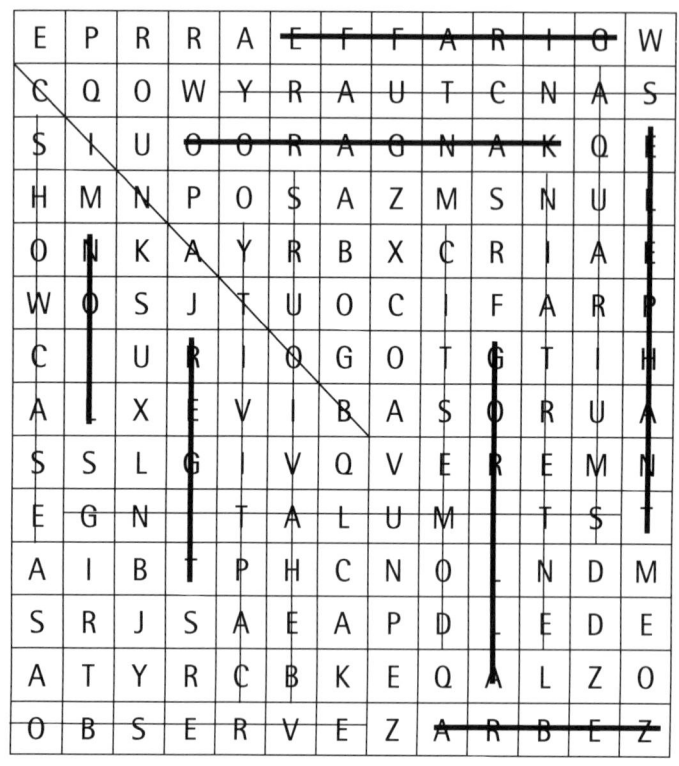

E	P	R	R	A	E	F	F	A	R	I	G	W
C	Q	O	W	Y	R	A	U	T	C	N	A	S
S	I	U	O	O	R	A	G	N	A	K	Q	E
H	M	N	P	O	S	A	Z	M	S	N	U	L
O	N	K	A	Y	R	B	X	C	R	I	A	E
W	O	S	J	T	U	O	C	I	F	A	R	P
C	U	R	I	O	G	O	T	G	T	I	H
A	X	E	V	B	A	S	O	R	U	A
S	S	L	G	V	Q	V	E	R	E	M	N
E	G	N	T	A	L	U	M	T	S	T
A	I	B	T	P	H	C	N	O	L	N	D	M
S	R	J	S	A	E	A	P	D	L	E	D	E
A	T	Y	R	C	B	K	E	Q	A	L	Z	O
O	B	S	E	R	V	E	Z	A	R	B	E	Z

(b) (i) sanctuary—place or time for preservation of birds and wild animals
(ii) domestic—kept by or living with people
(iii) botanic—pertaining to the study of the structure, physiology, classification and distribution of plants
(c) (i) elephant (ii) lion (iii) giraffe (iv) zebra (v) kangaroo (vi) gorilla (vii) tiger

2. (a) 'Showcasing' is a word used to describe the way in which people can see and learn about animals.
(b) (i) Zoos are useful for scientists as they are a way to gain a better understanding of the living needs of animals, such as habitat, diet and how they reproduce and raise their young.
(ii) Information gained by scientists assists conservationists so that they can provide suitable care for animals who have been orphaned or injured and cannot survive in the wild on their own, or for them to create an environment in which the animal can make a successful transition back into the wild.
(c) (i) They provide medical help for injured and orphaned animals before returning them to the sea.
(ii) They educate visitors on the problems faced by sea life.

Objectives

- Identifies and understands the meaning of new words.
- Extracts relevant information about modern zoos and wildlife parks.

Curriculum links

Country	Subject	Level	Objectives
England	Literacy	Year 5	• Spell words and group words according to their meanings.
		Year 6	• Spell familiar words correctly and employ strategies to spell difficult words.
Northern Ireland	Language and literacy	KS 2	• Acquire and develop a vocabulary.
Republic of Ireland	English	5th/6th Class	• Extend and develop vocabulary and spelling.
Scotland	English	Level D/E	• Know specialist vocabulary from different curricular areas.
Wales	English	KS 2	• Use their knowledge gained from reading to develop their vocabulary.

Look at us now!

1. **Complete these activities.**

   (a) Find each new word in the puzzle.

   New words
   - aquariums
   - behaviours
   - observe
   - botanic
   - domestic
   - entertain
   - stimulating
   - showcase
   - sanctuary
   - captivity

E	P	R	R	A	E	F	F	A	R	I	G	W
C	Q	O	W	Y	R	A	U	T	C	N	A	S
S	I	U	O	O	R	A	G	N	A	K	Q	E
H	M	N	P	O	S	A	Z	M	S	N	U	L
O	N	K	A	Y	R	B	X	C	R	I	A	E
W	O	S	J	T	U	O	C	I	F	A	R	P
C	I	U	R	I	O	G	O	T	G	T	I	H
A	L	X	E	V	I	B	A	S	O	R	U	A
S	S	L	G	I	V	Q	V	E	R	E	M	N
E	G	N	I	T	A	L	U	M	I	T	S	T
A	I	B	T	P	H	C	N	O	L	N	D	M
S	R	J	S	A	E	A	P	D	L	E	D	E
A	T	Y	R	C	B	K	E	Q	A	L	Z	O
O	B	S	E	R	V	E	Z	A	R	B	E	Z

   (b) Write meanings for these words. Use a dictionary to help you.

   (i) sanctuary _____

   (ii) domestic _____

   (iii) botanic _____

   (c) There are seven animals hidden in the puzzle which can be found at many zoos and safari parks. Can you find them?

   (i) e_____
   (ii) l_____
   (iii) g_____
   (iv) z_____
   (v) k_____
   (vi) g_____
   (vii) t_____

2. **Answer these questions.**

   (a) What is meant by 'showcasing' animals?
   _____

   (b) (i) How are zoos useful for scientists?
   _____

   (ii) How can the information gained by scientists help people caring for wildlife in conservation parks?
   _____

   (c) Write two main functions of the sea life sanctuaries.

   (i) _____

   (ii) _____

Teachers notes
Look at us now!

Answers
1. Teacher check
2. Answers will vary

Additional activities
- Build a miniature enclosure to suit an animal of your choice. Attempt to simulate its natural environment and include opportunities for providing stimulation for the animal.
- Brainstorm some of the difficulties zoo keepers may face keeping animals in captivity.

Lesson outline
- Discuss home renovation programmes and why things need to be changed. What kinds of things are changed? How do these things make living better for the people living in the house? Introduce the idea of renovating an animal enclosure. Discuss some things which could be changed to make the living conditions of an animal in captivity better.
- Read together the introduction at the top of the pupil activity page. Explain that the pupils are to pretend they are a renovation squad and need to 'make over' each of the enclosures in Question 1 to improve the living conditions of the animals and to make the enclosures simulate the natural environment of each.
- Allow the pupils to draw their make-over plans to complete Question 1.
- Discuss what is meant by 'stimulation'. Ask the pupils to share what it feels like to be bored, times and places they have felt bored and what they thought they would rather be doing at the time.
- Break the class into small groups or pairs and invite the pupils to think about what could be added to each animal's enclosure to stimulate it.
- Have the pupils use the ideas from their discussion to complete Question 2.

Objectives
- Designs animal enclosures that simulate each animal's environment.
- Suggests suitable stimulation for specific animals in captivity.

Curriculum links

Country	Subject	Level	Objectives
England	Science	KS 2	• Know how animals are suited to their environment.
Northern Ireland	Science and technology	KS 2	• Know about relationship between animals and plants in a habitat.
Republic of Ireland	Science	5th/6th Class	• Observe and explore some ways in which animal behaviour is influenced by, or adapted to, environmental conditions.
Scotland	Science	Level D	• Give examples of how animals are suited to their environment.
Wales	Science	KS 2	• Know how animals are suited to their environment.

Look at us now!

Room for improvement

What happens in zoos today is quite different from what happened there years ago. Once, zoos were simply a place people could go to see animals from their own and other countries. Today, they are a sanctuary for sick and endangered animals where scientists can work to develop breeding programmes to help species survive. To do this, the animals' enclosures have had to change to simulate the environments of each individual species.

1. Transform these enclosures to make them more suitable for each species. Label your drawings.

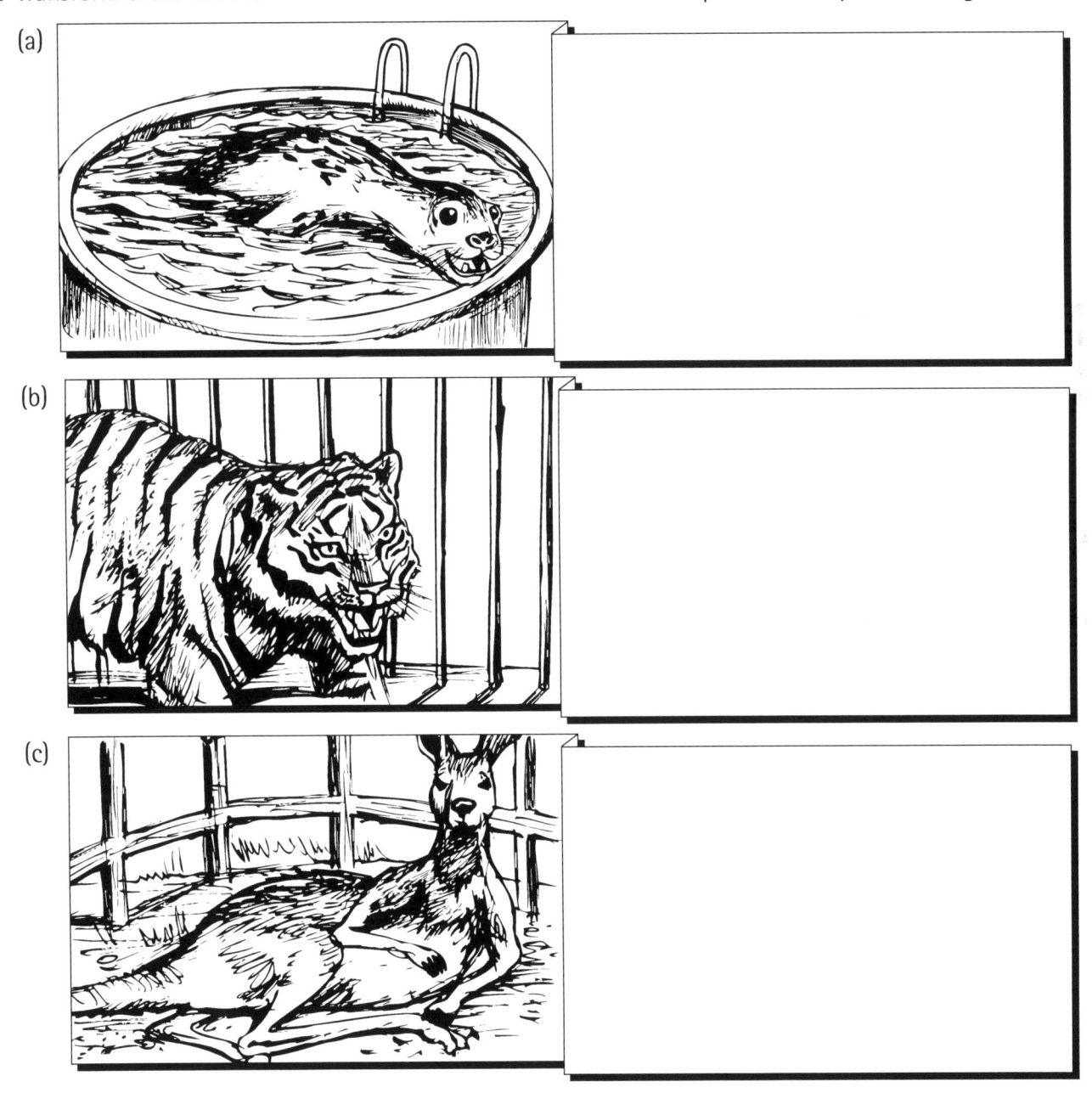

   (a)

   (b)

   (c)

2. Suggest a way each species might be stimulated to behave the way it would in the wild.

   (a) seal _____

   (b) tiger _____

   (c) kangaroo _____

Prim-Ed Publishing   www.prim-ed.com   **The environment**   87

Teachers notes
Look at us now!

Lesson outline

- Read together the information at the top of the pupil activity page. If possible, provide information 'plaques' for the pupils to view. (These may simply be exerts taken from an encyclopaedia, enlarged and mounted.)

- Direct the pupils to look at the categories on the plaque in Question 1. Explain that rather than filling out the information for an animal, the pupils must imagine that they themselves are the species being described and must complete their personalised plaques.

- Allow the pupils to complete their personalised plaques.

- Read together Question 2 (a), (b) and (c) and have the pupils highlight their opinions to state whether or not a suitable enclosure could be made for them based on this information and whether or not it could be as good as living in their current environment.

- Allow the pupils to complete Question 2 (d) independently and to share their reasons with the class about why they would or would not like to be kept in an enclosure.

- Allow the pupils to write their opinion to Question 2 (e). Discuss with the pupils the alternative some species face if not kept in enclosures for the purpose of breeding and protection.

Answers

1. Answers will vary
2. Answers will vary

Additional activities

- Research a native animal. Complete the plaque for the animal you chose.
- Visit a place where animals are kept in captivity. Evaluate the appropriateness of their enclosures. If this is not possible, evaluate the living conditions of your pets or the pets of someone you know.

Objective
- Writes an information plaque about a specific species.

Curriculum links

Country	Subject	Level	Objectives
England	Literacy	Year 5	Adapt non-narrative forms and styles to write factual texts.
Northern Ireland	Language and literacy	KS 2	Write using a variety of forms; e.g. reports.
Republic of Ireland	English	5th/6th Class	Write in a wide variety of genres; e.g. reports.
Scotland	English	Level C	Complete non-narrative writing in the context of other curricular areas.
Wales	English	KS 2	Write in non-fiction forms; e.g. reports.

Look at us now!

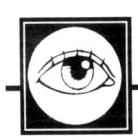

Information for change

Zoos are a great place to learn about animals. When we go to zoos or wildlife parks there are information plaques to inform visitors of the special attributes of each animal. This information helps us understand why the species is important and the reasons why it may be threatened in the wild.

1. Imagine you are a species being kept at a zoo or wildlife park. What would a zoologist or park ranger write on your plaque to go on display at your enclosure? Complete the plaque below.

Species name:

Physical description:

Behaviour:

Natural habitat:

Diet:

Special needs:

Threats:

2. (a) Do you think a scientist would be able to develop a suitable enclosure for you based on this information?

    Yes | No

    (b) How would it be different?

    _____

    _____

    (c) Do you agree with keeping animals in enclosures?   Yes | No

    Why?

    _____

    _____

    _____

    (d) Do you think it would be possible to build an enclosure for you which would be just as good as being in your normal environment?

    Yes | No

    (e) Do you think you would like to be kept in an enclosure?

    Yes | No

    Why?

    _____

    _____

    _____

Prim-Ed Publishing   www.prim-ed.com   **The environment**

Teachers notes
Getting your hands dirty

Background information

One of the best ways to encourage people into action about protecting the environment is to expand on the individual benefits rather than just continually emphasising the plight of threatened species and the world environment at large. It is true that in this day of advanced electronic media we have a better understanding of our place in the world and how everything is connected. Most people are now becoming aware that it is the responsibility of everyone, not just the scientists, to maintain a cleaner world.

Getting involved in creating a better garden environment for wildlife, or by participating in Clean-Up the World Day or vegetation regeneration, gives people something they can see as being a positive step in the right direction. Even better is the aesthetic value of a cleaner, greener environment to live in. By making the world's environment better for the benefit of all living things, life can be enhanced for every individual by providing more pleasant surroundings.

The practices that young people are now learning through classroom and community education will hopefully form a pattern for a cleaner, greener way of living. By participating in simple activities, pupils will learn skills and ethics to help them make environmentally-considerate choices in their adult life, from what type of washing machine they buy through to where they invest their savings.

Discussion points

- Why would you want to do the things in the '10 great ideas list'? What could motivate you to get involved?
- Do you think the problems people have caused for the Earth can be reversed? Or is it too late?

Websites

http://www.wwf.org
http://www.worldenvironmentday.org
http://www.cleanuptheworld.org
http://www.treecouncil.org.uk

Objective

- Reads and understands informational text about ways he/she can get involved in sustaining the environment.

Curriculum links

Country	Subject	Level	Objectives
England	Literacy	Year 5	• Use evidence from a text to explain events or ideas.
		Year 6	• Understand underlying themes, causes and points of view.
Northern Ireland	Language and literacy	KS 2	• Engage in a range of reading activities.
Republic of Ireland	English	5th/6th Class	• Explore non-fiction texts and use comprehension skills.
Scotland	English	Level D	• Complete practical reading tasks.
Wales	English	KS 2	• Read for information.

Getting your hands dirty

Every day, animals are losing their homes and their food supply. Every day, old-growth trees are being cut down and houses are built in their place. Every day in many places we never see, often far from our homes, thousands of trees and other vegetation are being cleared to provide land for crops and grazing.

Just one tree can be the host for many animals; for example, a single oak tree with lots of hollows may provide a home and nesting place for squirrels, rats, mice, birds, spiders, butterflies, moths, beetles and other insects.

It's time for us to take protecting our environment seriously! Now, you are probably sitting in your classroom, reading this, and thinking—'How can I possibly help? What can someone my age do?' Well ... here are ten great ideas to get you started—

1. Start a scrapbook of all the interesting facts you can find about wildlife.
2. Explore the Internet for information about wildlife and environmental issues—here are a few sites to start with:
   http://www.wwf.org
   (World Wide Fund for Nature)

   http://www.worldenvironmentday.org
   (World Environment Day)

   http://www.cleanuptheworld.org
   (Clean Up the World Day)
3. Look in the library for books on threatened species and conservation.
4. Ask your teacher if your class can plant some bird-attracting native shrubs in the school grounds, with the help of your school caretaker.
5. Ask your parents if you can plant a couple of native shrubs in your garden at home and make it your job to water and care for the plants.
6. Keep your pets inside, especially at night, to protect wildlife.
7. Place a bird water bowl high above the ground where cats cannot reach. Refill it daily. Perhaps also put some seed out for birds from time to time.
8. Become a junior member of a conservation group, like the World Wide Fund for Nature.
9. Participate in Clean-Up the World Day.
10. Fundraise for the local wildlife care group.

And to get your hands really dirty, when your local landcare group is having its next tree-planting day, ask your parents if they would like to be involved, and you can help plant trees too.

Just remember, every effort we make to improve the environment doesn't just help animals, it helps us too. The landscape will look better, we will have cleaner air and waterways and there will be more wildlife.

Teachers notes
Getting your hands dirty

Answers

1. (a) and (c)

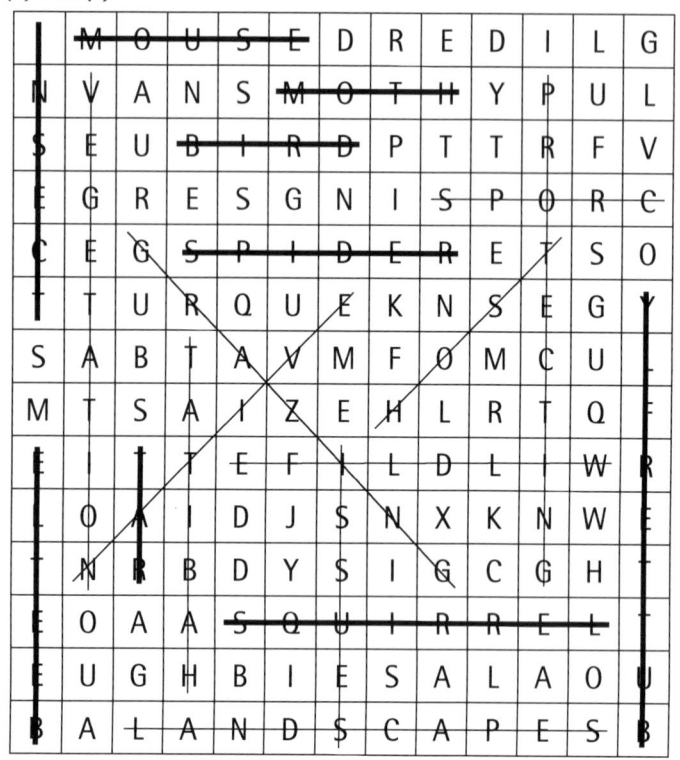

I	M̶	O̶	U̶	S̶	E̶	D	R	E	D	I	L	G
N	V	A	N	S	M̶	O̶	T̶	H̶	Y	P	U	L
S	E	U	B̶	I̶	R̶	D̶	P	T	T	R	F	V
E	G	R	E	S	G	N	I	S̶	P̶	O̶	R̶	C̶
C	E	G	S̶	P̶	I̶	D̶	E̶	R̶	E	T	S	O
T	T	U	R	Q	U	E	K	N	S	E	G	Y
S	A	B	T	A	V	M	F	O	M	C	U	F
M	T	S	A	I	Z	E	H	L	R	T	Q	F
E	I	I	T	E̶	F̶	I̶	L̶	D̶	L̶	I̶	W̶	R
E	O	A	I	D	J	S	N	X	K	N	W	E
E	N	R	B	D	Y	S	I	G	C	G	H	E
E	E	O	A	A	S̶	Q̶	U̶	I̶	R̶	R̶	E̶	L̶
E	E	U	G	H	B	I	E	S	A	L	A	O	U
B	A	L̶	A̶	N̶	D̶	S̶	C̶	A̶	P̶	E̶	S̶	B

   (b) (i) native—indigenous animal or plant
   (ii) wildlife—wild animals collectively
   (iii) host—one who entertains another

   (c) (i) squirrel (ii) rat (iii) mouse/moth (iv) bird (v) spider
   (vi) butterfly (vii) moth/mouse (viii) beetle (ix) insect

2. (a) (i) A 'host' provides for the needs of others.
   (ii) A tree can be a host by providing things such as shelter and food for animals.
   (b) (i) Answers will vary
   (ii) Answers will vary
   (c) Teacher check
   (d) 'Getting your hands dirty' means getting actively involved in bringing about a change for the better.

Objectives

- Identifies and understands the meaning of new words.
- Extracts relevant information about sustaining the environment.

Curriculum links

Country	Subject	Level	Objectives
England	Literacy	Year 5	• Spell words and group words according to their meanings.
		Year 6	• Spell familiar words correctly and employ strategies to spell difficult words.
Northern Ireland	Language and literacy	KS 2	• Acquire and develop a vocabulary.
Republic of Ireland	English	5th/6th Class	• Extend and develop vocabulary and spelling.
Scotland	English	Level D/E	• Know specialist vocabulary from different curricular areas.
Wales	English	KS 2	• Use their knowledge gained from reading to develop their vocabulary.

Getting your hands dirty

1. **Complete these activities.**

   (a) Find each new word in the puzzle.

   New words
   - vegetation
   - crops
   - host
   - protecting
   - native
   - habitat
   - grazing
   - landscape
   - issues
   - wildlife

I	M	O	U	S	E	D	R	E	D	I	L	G
N	V	A	N	S	M	O	T	H	Y	P	U	L
S	E	U	B	I	R	D	P	T	T	R	F	V
E	G	R	E	S	G	N	I	S	P	O	R	C
C	E	G	S	P	I	D	E	R	E	T	S	O
T	T	U	R	Q	U	E	K	N	S	E	G	Y
S	A	B	T	A	V	M	F	O	M	C	U	L
M	T	S	A	I	Z	E	H	L	R	T	Q	F
E	I	T	T	E	F	I	L	D	L	I	W	R
L	O	A	I	D	J	S	N	X	K	N	W	E
T	N	R	B	D	Y	S	I	G	C	G	H	T
E	O	A	A	S	Q	U	I	R	R	E	L	T
E	U	G	H	B	I	E	S	A	L	A	O	U
B	A	L	A	N	D	S	C	A	P	E	S	B

   (b) Write meanings for these words. Use a dictionary to help you.

   (i) native _____

   (ii) wildlife _____

   (iii) host _____

   (c) There are nine extra words hidden in the puzzle. They are the names of creatures which might all live in one oak tree.

   (i) sq_____
   (ii) r_____
   (iii) m_____
   (iv) bi_____
   (v) sp_____
   (vi) bu_____
   (vii) m_____
   (viii) be_____
   (ix) i_____

2. **Answer these questions.**

   (a) (i) What does a 'host' do? _____

   (ii) How can a tree be a host? _____

   (b) (i) Name the environmental website you would most like to visit.

   _____

   (ii) What do you think you might find out about at this site?

   _____

   (c) Circle the things in the top ten list you want to do to help save the environment.

   (d) What do you think the author means by 'getting your hands dirty'?

   _____

Teachers notes
Getting your hands dirty

Answers
1. Answers will vary
2. Answers will vary
3. Answers will vary
4. Answers will vary

Additional activities
- Create a native habitat by planting native trees and attracting birds and other wildlife.
- Find out what used to be where the school is now. Brainstorm how the previous habitat was disturbed for the school to be built. Evaluate the impact building the school had on the environment.

Lesson outline
- Encourage the pupils to share some of their hobbies with the class. Discuss why they enjoy them, how often they do them and who they share them with. Introduce the idea of being an environmentalist as a hobby. What kinds of things would you do? How often would you do them and who would you share them with?

- Read together the information about attracting wildlife at the top of the pupil activity page. Suggest that projects such as these are examples of what environmentalists do.

- Read Question 1 and encourage the pupils to research this information. They could ask people in the local area, visit the library to find out what types of plants do well in the ecosystem which now exists or which existed before the school was built.

- Pool the information gained from the pupils' investigations to complete Question 1.

- Take the pupils for a walk around the school or allow them to spend 5 minutes roaming the school in search of an ideal location for creating a 'native' habitat. Have them return and write a description of the location they found and why they think it would be suitable for a natural environment to complete Question 2.

- Allow the pupils to read and complete Question 3 independently and to read the information which follows.

- As a whole class, review the importance of trees. In particular, revise the process of photosynthesis and how it is vital for the sustainability of humans. Brainstorm a list of other benefits from having trees for animals and plants and for humans. Think from both a practical and an aesthetic point of view.

- Have the pupils use ideas from the class brainstorm to complete Question 4.

Objectives
- Researches to locate plants native to his or her local environment.
- Suggests ways to encourage animals to inhabit an area.
- Suggests how tree planting creates a better environment.

Curriculum links

Country	Subject	Level	Objectives
England	Geography	KS 2	• Recognise how and why people may seek to manage environments sustainably and identify opportunities for their own involvement.
Northern Ireland	Geography	KS 2	• Know about the importance of conserving natural resources and ways in which people conserve the environment.
Republic of Ireland	Geography/ Science	5th/6th Class	• Come to appreciate individual and community responsibility for environmental care.
Scotland	Science	Level D	• Describe examples of human impact on the environment that have brought about beneficial changes and detrimental changes.
Wales	Geography	KS 2	• Understand the individual's responsibility for the environment.

Getting your hands dirty

Attracting wildlife

You can begin helping the environment in your own garden or in your school grounds by creating a habitat for native birds and animals. To do this, you will need to find out what the native flora is (or was) in your local environment to make sure you choose plants suitable for the wildlife in your area.

1. Research and list some plants native to your area.

2. Where would be a good location to create a 'native' habitat?

   Why?

3. (a) What types of animals would you like to attract to the 'native' habitat?

   (b) What else could you do to encourage this type of animal to live in your 'native' habitat?

Creating a 'native' garden is a small step towards helping to rebuild the natural habitats of all wildlife.

4. Brainstorm how planting trees is also helping create a better environment for us to live in.

Teachers notes
Getting your hands dirty

Lesson outline

- Introduce the word 'media'. What is the job of people involved in the media? What forms of communication do they use to get their information to the public?
- Read together the information at the top of the pupil activity page about environmental issues in the media.
- Provide newspapers for the pupils to peruse. Allow them to highlight any articles they find about the environment and encourage them to summarise and share briefly the content of the article with the class.
- Have the pupils write a short sentence describing three or four of the articles shared to complete Question 1.
- Invite the pupils to read and complete Question 2 by circling an issue of importance to them in the list above.
- Allow the pupils to read and complete Question 3 about the issue they chose independently. To assist the pupils to complete this task, allow them to review the article about their issue.
- Provide a number of colour flyers or posters for the pupils to view and evaluate. Have them comment upon which were most eye-catching and successful in getting their message across. Have the pupils design a flyer or poster of their own in the space provided in Question 4. Their design should be a simple layout and should not include the detail that will be included in their final flyer. Emphasise that their design drawing is merely a draft to ensure the colours and design will grab the attention of the public, and to note keywords and phrases.
- Allow the pupils time to make their flyers. Provide ample resources and encourage the pupils to be as creative, but as simple, as they can.
- Display the pupils' flyers around the school grounds to encourage awareness of environmental issues.

Answers

1. Answers will vary
2. Teacher check
3. Answers will vary
4. Teacher check

Additional activities

- Identify places around the school or in the local community where your poster would be most visible and have the greatest impact.
- Become an environmentalist and make a conscious decision to care for the environment. Start a school environmental club and hold a tree planting day in the school as an inauguration.

Objectives

- Identifies environmental issues in the media.
- Designs a poster to promote sustaining the environment.

Curriculum links

Country	Subject	Level	Objectives
England	PSHE	KS 2	Explore how the media present information.
Northern Ireland	PD	KS 2	Explore how the media present information.
Republic of Ireland	SPHE	5th/6th Class	Explore the role of newspapers and other forms of print media in transmitting messages.
Scotland	Health	Level D	Recognise that media influences can affect choices they make.
Wales	PSHE	KS 2	Be concerned about the environment.

Getting your hands dirty

In the media

There are many environmental issues being discussed in the media. In most cases, it is people who have to change the way they live, work and interact with their environment if the 'right thing' is going to be done for the environment.

1. List the environmental issues you know of or have heard or read about in the media.

2. Circle the issues in the box above that you believe you can do something to help.

3. Choose one of the issues you circled and answer the following questions.

    (a) What is the issue?

    (b) Why does the problem exist?

    (c) What will happen if the problem is not addressed?

    (d) What can we do to help solve the problem?

4. Use the information in Question 3 to make a poster on a separate sheet of paper or card. Remember to use eye-catching colours, short simple statements or bullet points, and to encourage people in a positive way to help save our environment! Draw a plan of your poster design below.

Glossary

Aerosol – a substance sealed in a container under pressure and released as a fine spray

Agriculture – the science or practice of farming

Alpine – relating to or growing on high mountains

Alternative – one of two or more available

Amphibian – cold-blooded animal, such as a frog or toad, which lives in the water when young and on the land as an adult

Ancient – belonging to the very distant past – very old

Aquarium – water-filled glass tank for keeping fish, other water creatures, and plants

Arid – very dry because of having little or no rain

Artificial – made as a copy of something natural

Atmosphere – the gases surrounding the earth, or another planet

Behaviour – the way in which someone or something behaves (functions)

Biodiversity – the variety of plant and animal life in the world or in a habitat

Botanical – relating to botany, the scientific study of plants

Breeding – mating and producing young

By-product – a product produced in the making of something else

Capital – wealth

Captive – confined – not free to choose an alternative

Carbon dioxide (CO_2) - a gas produced by burning carbon and by breathing, and absorbed by plants in photosynthesis

Chlorofluorocarbon (CFC) – gas compound of carbon, hydrogen, chlorine and fluorine – used in old refrigerators and aerosols and harmful to the ozone layer of the atmosphere

Coastal wetlands – swampy or marshy land found on or near the coastline

Commercial – making or intended to make a profit

Community – a group of animals or plants living or growing in the same place

Competition – the activity of competing against others

Compost – decayed organic material, often used as fertiliser

Conservation – preservation or restoration of the natural environment

Conservationist – a person involved in preserving or restoring the natural environment

Cropping – growing plants for food or other use

Damage – physical harm reducing the value or usefulness of something

Decline – become smaller, weaker or worse

Degradation – the action of being broken down or made worse

Derived – obtained or originated from

Destroy – cause something to cease to exist by badly damaging it

Destruction – the action of destroying something so that it ceases to exist

Disturbed – interfered with the normal arrangement or functioning of things

Diversity – a range of different things, being varied

Domestic (of an animal) – tame and kept by humans

Glossary

Drought – a very long period of little or no rainfall

Ecosystem – a community of organisms interacting with each other and their non-living environment

Environment – the surroundings in which a person, animal or plant lives

Estimate – an approximate calculation

Extinct – a species having no living members; i.e. no longer in existence

Extinction spasm – a sudden brief time in which species are being driven to extinction – i.e. having no living members, ceasing to exist

Extract – obtain a substance or resource from something by a special method

Fertiliser – a chemical or natural substance added to the soil to increase its fertility

Fossil fuels – coal, petroleum or natural gas, a non-renewable energy source that formed long ago from remains of swamp forests

Free-range (livestock or eggs) – kept or produced in natural conditions, where the animals may move around freely

Gases – air-like substances which expand to fill any space available

Geothermal – relating to or produced by the internal heat of the Earth

Global warming – the gradual increase in the overall temperature of the earth's atmosphere due to (suspected) increased levels of carbon dioxide and other pollutants

Grazing – grassland suitable for use as pasture for livestock (e.g. cattle, sheep)

Greenhouse effect – overall warming of the earth's lower atmosphere, caused by radiation (heat) from the sun being trapped by gases such as carbon dioxide

Habitat destruction – destroying the place where an organism or species normally lives

Headquarters – the centre of an organisation from where activities are directed

Humidity – the amount of moisture (water) in the air

Illegal – against the law

Income – money received during a certain period of work

Industry – the manufacture of goods in factories

International – existing or occurring between nations

Introduce – insert or bring into a place for the first time

Invertebrate – an animal without a backbone; e.g. insects. Of the 2 million named species in the animal kingdom, all but 50 000 are invertebrates.

Latin – the language of ancient Rome and its empire. Dead language no longer spoken by any country as its normal language. Often used for terms in science and medicine.

Glossary

Lifestyle – the way in which someone lives

Loggers – workers whose job it is to cut down trees for use in the timber industry

Mammal – a warm-blooded animal that has hair or fur, produces milk, and bears live young

Marine – relating to the sea

Methane – a flammable gas which is the main component of natural gas

Mineral – a solid inorganic substance occurring naturally, e.g. copper

Mollusc – invertebrate animal (no backbone) belonging to a large group including snails, slugs and mussels. Soft-bodied and often has an external shell.

Mulch – a mass of leaves, bark or compost which can enrich the soil

National – characteristic of a particular nation (country)

Natural – existing in or obtained from nature; not made or caused by humans

Old growth forest – forests where trees are old enough to have developed hollows; i.e. between 100 and 500 years old

Organisation – an organised group of people with a particular purpose; e.g. business

Orphan – an offspring whose parents have died

Over-harvesting (re fishing industry) – when stocks of fish are caught at levels higher than the fish can naturally repopulate

Plantation – an area in which trees have been planted as a crop

Poaching – taking (animals) illegally from private or protected areas

Poison – a substance that causes death or injury when swallowed or absorbed by a living organism

Polar icecaps – permanent covering of ice over large areas at the North and South Poles

Pollution – substances that are harmful or poisonous

Population – number of people or other species of a particular place

Preserve – keep in its original or existing state

Products – articles or substances manufactured for sale

Recycling – converting waste into a form in which it can be reused

Reduce – make or become less

Re-establish – re-start or bring about again

Renewable energy – capable of being restored to its original state when used

Reproduce – produce offspring

Reptiles – cold-blooded vertebrate animals including snakes, lizards, crocodiles and turtles

Reserve – keep for future use

Resource – a supply of materials that can be drawn on when needed

Restore – return to previous condition

Result – a thing that is caused or produced by something else; an outcome

Reuse – use again or more than once

Sanctuary – nature reserve; a place where injured or unwanted animals are cared for

Sapling – a young, slender tree

Glossary

Scientist – a person who has expert knowledge of one or more of the natural or physical sciences

Solar – having to do with the sun or its rays

Species – a group of animals or plants consisting of similar individuals capable of breeding with each other

Survival – being able to continue to live or exist

Sustain – keep something continuing over time

Technology – practical or mechanical sciences used in industry

Terrestrial (of an animal or a plant) – living on or in the ground (i.e. not aquatic)

Threatened – being put at risk

Timber – wood prepared for use in building and carpentry

Trade – the buying and selling of goods and services

Treaty – a formal signed agreement between states (countries)

Tropical – very hot and humid areas within the tropics (the region between the Tropic of Capricorn and the Tropic of Cancer)

Vegetation – plants in general

Waste – discarded matter that is no longer useful or required

Wildlife – the native animals of a region

Zoo – a place which keeps wild animals for study, conservation or display to the public